CAMBRIDGE LIBRARY COLLECTION

Books of enduring scholarly value

English Men of Letters

In the 1870s, Macmillan publishers began to issue a series of books called 'English Men of Letters' – biographies of English writers by other English writers. The general editor of the series was the journalist, critic, politician, and supporter (and later biographer) of Gladstone, John Morley (1838–1923). The first volume published was Samuel Johnson, by Leslie Stephen (1878), and the first series (which continued until 1892) eventually consisted of 39 volumes. The aim was to provide a short introduction to each subject and his works, but also that the life should illuminate the works, and vice versa. All the subjects were men, as were all but one of the authors (Mrs Oliphant on Sheridan); and all but one (Hawthorne) were English or Irish. The subjects range chronologically from Chaucer to Thackeray and Dickens, and an important feature of the series is that many of the authors (Henry James on Hawthorne, Ward on Dickens) were discussing writers of the previous generation, and some (Trollope on Thackeray) had even known their subjects personally. The series exemplifies the British approach to literary biography and criticism at the end of the nineteenth century, and also reveals which authors were at that time regarded as canonical.

Goldsmith

Written by Scottish novelist William Black (1841–98), this biography of the Irish-born poet, dramatist and novelist Oliver Goldsmith (c.1728–74) was published in 1878 as the sixth book in the first series of English Men of Letters. Goldsmith is best known for his novel *The Vicar of Wakefield* (1766) and the play *She Stoops to Conquer* (1771), as well as his close association with Samuel Johnson, James Boswell, and William Hogarth. The biography is a colourful one: as Black observes, Goldsmith, who was trained as a physician but whose whole career was in literature, possessed a 'happy knack of enjoying the present hour', and his pursuit of pleasure frequently left him in debt. Black himself was one of the most prolific and popular writers of his day; a collected edition of his works published 1892–4 ran to twenty-six volumes.

Cambridge University Press has long been a pioneer in the reissuing of out-of-print titles from its own backlist, producing digital reprints of books that are still sought after by scholars and students but could not be reprinted economically using traditional technology. The Cambridge Library Collection extends this activity to a wider range of books which are still of importance to researchers and professionals, either for the source material they contain, or as landmarks in the history of their academic discipline.

Drawing from the world-renowned collections in the Cambridge University Library, and guided by the advice of experts in each subject area, Cambridge University Press is using state-of-the-art scanning machines in its own Printing House to capture the content of each book selected for inclusion. The files are processed to give a consistently clear, crisp image, and the books finished to the high quality standard for which the Press is recognised around the world. The latest print-on-demand technology ensures that the books will remain available indefinitely, and that orders for single or multiple copies can quickly be supplied.

The Cambridge Library Collection will bring back to life books of enduring scholarly value (including out-of-copyright works originally issued by other publishers) across a wide range of disciplines in the humanities and social sciences and in science and technology.

Goldsmith

WILLIAM BLACK

CAMBRIDGE UNIVERSITY PRESS

Cambridge, New York, Melbourne, Madrid, Cape Town,
Singapore, São Paolo, Delhi, Tokyo, Mexico City

Published in the United States of America by Cambridge University Press, New York

www.cambridge.org
Information on this title: www.cambridge.org/9781108034708

© in this compilation Cambridge University Press 2011

This edition first published 1878
This digitally printed version 2011

ISBN 978-1-108-03470-8 Paperback

English Men of Letters

EDITED BY JOHN MORLEY

GOLDSMITH

GOLDSMITH

BY

WILLIAM BLACK

London

MACMILLAN AND CO

1878

LONDON :

R. CLAY, SONS, AND TAYLOR, PRINTERS

BREAD STREET HILL.

CONTENTS.

CHAPTER VI.

CHAPTER VII.

CHAPTER VIII.

CHAPTER IX.

CHAPTER X.

CHAPTER XI.

CHAPTER XII.

CHAPTER XIII.

CHAPTER XIV.

CHAPTER XV

CHAPTER XVI.

CHAPTER XVII.

GOLDSMITH

CHAPTER I.

INTRODUCTORY.

"INNOCENTLY to amuse the imagination in this dream of life is wisdom." So wrote Oliver Goldsmith; and surely among those who have earned the world's gratitude by this ministration he must be accorded a conspicuous place. If, in these delightful writings of his, he mostly avoids the darker problems of existence—if the mystery of the tragic and apparently unmerited and unrequited suffering in the world is rarely touched upon—we can pardon the omission for the sake of the gentle optimism that would rather look on the kindly side of life. "You come hot and tired from the day's battle, and this sweet minstrel sings to you," says Mr. Thackeray. "Who could harm the kind vagrant harper? Whom did he ever hurt? He carries no weapon save the harp on which he plays to you; and with which he delights great and humble, young and old, the captains in the tents, or the soldiers round the

𝕴   B

fire, or the women and children in the villages, at whose
porches he stops and sings his simple songs of love and
beauty." And it is to be suspected—it is to be hoped,
at least—that the cheerfulness which shines like sun-
light through Goldsmith's writings, did not altogether
desert himself even in the most trying hours of his
wayward and troubled career. He had, with all his
sensitiveness, a fine happy-go-lucky disposition; was
ready for a frolic when he had a guinea, and, when he
had none, could turn a sentence on the humorous side
of starvation; and certainly never attributed to the
injustice or neglect of society misfortunes the origin
of which lay nearer home.

Of course, a very dark picture might be drawn of
Goldsmith's life; and the sufferings that he undoubtedly
endured have been made a whip with which to lash the
ingratitude of a world not too quick to recognise the
claims of genius. He has been put before us, without
any brighter lights to the picture, as the most unfortunate of poor devils; the heart-broken usher; the
hack ground down by sordid booksellers; the starving
occupant of successive garrets. This is the aspect of
Goldsmith's career which naturally attracts Mr. Forster.
Mr. Forster seems to have been haunted throughout his
life by the idea that Providence had some especial spite
against literary persons; and that, in a measure to com-
pensate them for their sad lot, society should be very kind
to them, while the Government of the day might make
them Companions of the Bath or give them posts in the
Civil Service. In the otherwise copious, thorough, and
valuable *Life and Times of Oliver Goldsmith*, we find an
almost humiliating insistance on the complaint that

Oliver Goldsmith did not receive greater recognition
and larger sums of money from his contemporaries.
Goldsmith is here "the poor neglected sizar"; his
"marked ill-fortune" attends him constantly; he shares
"the evil destinies of men of letters"; he was one of
those who "struggled into fame without the aid of
English institutions"; in short, "he wrote, and paid the
penalty." Nay, even Christianity itself is impeached
on account of the persecution suffered by poor Goldsmith. "There had been a Christian religion extant
for seventeen-hundred and fifty-seven years," writes Mr.
Forster, "the world having been acquainted, for even so
long, with its spiritual necessities and responsibilities;
yet here, in the middle of the eighteenth century, was
the eminence ordinarily conceded to a spiritual teacher,
to one of those men who come upon the earth to lift
their fellow-men above its miry ways. He is up in a
garret, writing for bread he cannot get, and dunned for
a milk-score he cannot pay." That Christianity might
have been worse employed than in paying the milkman's
score is true enough, for then the milkman would have
come by his own; but that Christianity, or the state, or
society should be scolded because an author suffers the
natural consequences of his allowing his expenditure
to exceed his income, seems a little hard. And this is
a sort of writing that is peculiarly inappropriate in
the case of Goldsmith, who, if ever any man was author
of his own misfortunes, may fairly have the charge
brought against him. "Men of genius," says Mr.
Forster, "can more easily starve, than the world, with
safety to itself, can continue to neglect and starve
them." Perhaps so; but the English nation, which

has always had a regard and even love for Oliver Goldsmith, that is quite peculiar in the history of literature,
and which has been glad to overlook his faults and
follies, and eager to sympathise with him in the many
miseries of his career, will be slow to believe that it
is responsible for any starvation that Goldsmith may
have endured.

However, the key-note has been firmly struck, and it
still vibrates. Goldsmith was the unluckiest of mortals,
the hapless victim of circumstances. "Yielding to that
united pressure of labour, penury, and sorrow, with
a frame exhausted by unremitting and ill-rewarded
drudgery, Goldsmith was indebted to the forbearance
of creditors for a peaceful burial." But what, now,
if some foreigner strange to the traditions of English
literature—some Japanese student, for example, or the
New Zealander come before his time—were to go over
the ascertained facts of Goldsmith's life, and were
suddenly to announce to us, with the happy audacity
of ignorance, that he, Goldsmith, was a quite ex-
ceptionally fortunate person? "Why," he might say, "I
find that in a country where the vast majority of people
are born to labour, Oliver Goldsmith was never asked
to do a stroke of work towards the earning of his own
living until he had arrived at man's estate. All that
was expected of him, as a youth and as a young man,
was that he should equip himself fully for the battle of
life. He was maintained at college until he had taken
his degree. Again and again he was furnished with
funds for further study and foreign travel; and again
and again he gambled his opportunities away. The
constant kindness of his uncle only made him the best

begging-letter-writer the world has seen. In the midst
of his debt and distress as a bookseller's drudge, he
receives £400 for three nights' performance of *The
Good-Natured Man ;* he immediately purchases chambers
in Brick Court for £400 ; and forthwith begins to
borrow as before. It is true that he died owing £2000,
and was indebted to the forbearance of creditors for a
peaceful burial ; but it appears that during the last
seven years of his life he had been earning an annual
income equivalent to £800 of English currency.[1] He
was a man liberally and affectionately brought up, who
had many relatives and many friends, and who had the
proud satisfaction—which has been denied to many men
of genius—of knowing for years before he died that his
merits as a writer had been recognised by the great
bulk of his countrymen. And yet this strange English
nation is inclined to suspect that it treated him rather
badly ; and Christianity is attacked because it did not
pay Goldsmith's milkscore."

Our Japanese friend may be exaggerating ; but his
position is after all fairly tenable. It may at least
be looked at, before entering on the following brief
résumé of the leading facts in Goldsmith's life, if only
to restore our equanimity. For, naturally, it is not
pleasant to think that any previous generation, however
neglectful of the claims of literary persons (as com-
pared with the claims of such wretched creatures as
physicians, men of science, artists, engineers, and so

[1] The calculation is Lord Macaulay's : see his *Biographical
Essays.*

forth) should so cruelly have ill-treated one whom we all love now. This inheritance of ingratitude is more than we can bear. Is it true that Goldsmith was so harshly dealt with by those barbarian ancestors of ours?

CHAPTER II.

THE Goldsmiths were of English descent; Goldsmith's father was a Protestant clergyman in a poor little village in the county of Longford; and when Oliver, one of several children, was born in this village of Pallas, or Pallasmore, on the 10th November, 1728, the Rev. Charles Goldsmith was passing rich on £40 a year. But a couple of years later Mr. Goldsmith succeeded to a more lucrative living; and forthwith removed his family to the village of Lissoy, in the county of Westmeath.

Here at once our interest in the story begins : is this Lissoy the sweet Auburn that we have known and loved since our childhood? Lord Macaulay, with a great deal of vehemence, avers that it is not; that there never was any such hamlet as Auburn in Ireland; that *The Deserted Village* is a hopelessly incongruous poem; and that Goldsmith, in combining a description of a probably Kentish village with a description of an Irish ejectment, "has produced something which never was, and never will be, seen in any part of the world." This criticism is ingenious and plausible, but it is unsound, for it happens to overlook one of

the radical facts of human nature—the magnifying
delight of the mind in what is long remembered and
remote. What was it that the imagination of Goldsmith,
in his life-long banishment, could not see when he
looked back to the home of his childhood, and his early
friends, and the sports and occupations of his youth?
Lissoy was no doubt a poor enough Irish village; and
perhaps the farms were not too well cultivated; and
perhaps the village preacher, who was so dear to all
the country round, had to administer many a thrashing
to a certain graceless son of his; and perhaps Paddy
Byrne was something of a pedant; and no doubt pigs
ran over the "nicely sanded floor" of the inn; and no
doubt the village statesmen occasionally indulged in
a free fight. But do you think that was the Lissoy that
Goldsmith thought of in his dreary lodgings in Fleet-
Street courts? No. It was the Lissoy where the
vagrant lad had first seen the "primrose peep beneath
the thorn"; where he had listened to the mysterious
call of the bittern by the unfrequented river; it was
a Lissoy still ringing with the glad laughter of young
people in the twilight hours; it was a Lissoy for ever
beautiful, and tender, and far away. The grown-up
Goldsmith had not to go to any Kentish village for a
model; the familiar scenes of his youth, regarded with
all the wistfulness and longing of an exile, became
glorified enough. "If I go to the opera where Signora
Colomba pours out all the mazes of melody," he writes
to Mr. Hodson, "I sit and sigh for Lissoy's fire-side,
and *Johnny Armstrong's Last Good Night* from Peggy
Golden."

There was but little in the circumstances of Gold-

smith's early life likely to fit him for, or to lead him
into, a literary career; in fact, he did not take to
literature until he had tried pretty nearly everything
else as a method of earning a living. If he was intended for anything, it was no doubt his father's
wish that he should enter the Church; and he got
such education as the poor Irish clergyman—who was
not a very provident person—could afford. The child
Goldsmith was first of all taught his alphabet at home,
by a maid-servant, who was also a relation of the family;
then, at the age of six, he was sent to that village school
which, with its profound and learned master, he has
made familiar to all of us; and after that he was sent
further a-field for his learning, being moved from this to
the other boarding-school as the occasion demanded.
Goldsmith's school-life could not have been altogether a
pleasant time for him. We hear, indeed, of his being
concerned in a good many frolics—robbing orchards,
and the like; and it is said that he attained proficiency
in the game of fives. But a shy and sensitive lad
like Goldsmith, who was eagerly desirous of being
thought well of, and whose appearance only invited the
thoughtless but cruel ridicule of his schoolmates, must
have suffered a good deal. He was little, pitted with
the small-pox, and awkward; and schoolboys are
amazingly frank. He was not strong enough to thrash
them into respect of him; he had no big brother to
become his champion; his pocket-money was not lavish
enough to enable him to buy over enemies or subsidise
allies.

In similar circumstances it has sometimes happened
that a boy physically inferior to his companions has

consoled himself by proving his mental prowess—has
scored off his failure at cricket by the taking of prizes, and
has revenged himself for a drubbing by writing a lampoon.
But even this last resource was not open to Goldsmith.
He was a dull boy; "a stupid, heavy blockhead," is
Dr. Strean's phrase in summing up the estimate formed
of young Goldsmith by his contemporaries at school.
Of course, as soon as he became famous, everybody
began to hunt up recollections of his having said or
done this or that, in order to prove that there were
signs of the coming greatness. People began to remember that he had been suspected of scribbling
verses, which he burned. What schoolboy has not
done the like? We know how the biographers of
great painters point out to us that their hero early
showed the bent of his mind by drawing the figures
of animals on doors and walls with a piece of chalk;
as to which it may be observed that, if every schoolboy
who scribbled verses and sketched in chalk on a brick
wall, were to grow up a genius, poems and pictures
would be plentiful enough. However, there is the
apparently authenticated anecdote of young Goldsmith's
turning the tables on the fiddler at his uncle's dancing-
party. The fiddler, struck by the odd look of the boy
who was capering about the room, called out "Æsop!"
whereupon Goldsmith is said to have instantly replied,

> "Our herald hath proclaimed this saying,
> See Æsop dancing and his monkey playing!"

But even if this story be true, it is worth nothing as an
augury; for quickness of repartee was precisely the ac-
complishment which the adult Goldsmith conspicuously

lacked. Put a pen into his hand, and shut him up in a room : then he was master of the situation— nothing could be more incisive, polished, and easy than his playful sarcasm. But in society any fool could get the better of him by a sudden question followed by a horse-laugh. All through his life—even after he had become one of the most famous of living writers— Goldsmith suffered from want of self-confidence. He was too anxious to please. In his eager acquiescence, he would blunder into any trap that was laid for him. A grain or two of the stolid self-sufficiency of the blockheads who laughed at him would not only have improved his character, but would have considerably added to the happiness of his life.

As a natural consequence of this timidity, Goldsmith, when opportunity served, assumed airs of magnificent importance. Every one knows the story of the mistake on which *She Stoops to Conquer* is founded. Getting free at last from all the turmoil, and anxieties, and mortifications of school-life, and returning home on a lent hack, the released schoolboy is feeling very grand indeed. He is now sixteen, would fain pass for a man, and has a whole golden guinea in his pocket. And so he takes the journey very leisurely until, getting be- nighted in a certain village, he asks the way to the " best house," and is directed by a facetious person to the house of the squire. The squire by good luck falls in with the joke ; and then we have a very pretty comedy indeed—the impecunious schoolboy playing the part of a fine gentleman on the strength of his solitary guinea, ordering a bottle of wine after his supper, and inviting his landlord and his landlord's wife and daughter

to join him in the supper-room. The contrast, in *She
Stoops to Conquer*, between Marlow's embarrassed diffi-
dence on certain occasions and his audacious effrontery
on others, found many a parallel in the incidents of
Goldsmith's own life; and it is not improbable that
the writer of the comedy was thinking of some of his
own experiences, when he made Miss Hardcastle say
to her timid suitor : " A want of courage upon some
occasions assumes the appearance of ignorance, and
betrays us when we most want to excel.''

It was, perhaps, just as well that the supper, and
bottle of wine, and lodging at Squire Featherston's had
not to be paid for out of the schoolboy's guinea; for
young Goldsmith was now on his way to college, and
the funds at the disposal of the Goldsmith family
were not over abundant.   Goldsmith's sister having
married the son of a well-to-do man, her father considered it a point of honour that she should have a
dowry : and in giving her a sum of £400 he so crippled
the means of the family, that Goldsmith had to be sent
to college not as a pensioner but as a sizar.   It appears
that the young gentleman's pride revolted against this
proposal; and that he was won over to consent only by
the persuasions of his uncle Contarine, who himself had
been a sizar.   So Goldsmith, now in his eighteenth year,
went to Dublin ; managed somehow or other—though
he was the last in the list—to pass the necessary examination ; and entered upon his college career (1745.)

How he lived, and what he learned, at Trinity College, are both largely matters of conjecture; the chief
features of such record as we have are the various
means of raising a little money to which the poor

sizar had to resort; a continual quarrelling with his
tutor, an ill-conditioned brute, who baited Goldsmith
and occasionally beat him; and a chance frolic when
funds were forthcoming.   It was while he was at
Trinity College that his father died; so that Goldsmith was rendered more than ever dependent on the
kindness of his uncle Contarine, who throughout seems
to have taken much interest in his odd, ungainly
nephew.   A loan from a friend or a visit to the
pawnbroker tided over the severer difficulties; and
then from time to time the writing of street-ballads,
for which he got five shillings a-piece at a certain
repository, came in to help.   It was a happy-go-lucky,
hand to-mouth sort of existence, involving a good deal
of hardship and humiliation, but having its frolics and
gaieties notwithstanding.   One of these was pretty near
to putting an end to his collegiate career altogether.
He had, smarting under a public admonition for having
been concerned in a riot, taken seriously to his studies
and had competed for a scholarship.   He missed the
scholarship, but gained an exhibition of the value of
thirty shillings; whereupon he collected a number of
friends of both sexes in his rooms, and proceeded to
have high jinks there.   In the midst of the dancing
and uproar, in comes his tutor, in such a passion that
he knocks Goldsmith down.   This insult, received
before his friends, was too much for the unlucky sizar,
who, the very next day, sold his books, ran away from
college, and ultimately, after having been on the verge
of starvation once or twice, made his way to Lissoy.
Here his brother got hold of him; persuaded him to
go back; and the escapade was condoned somehow.

Goldsmith remained at Trinity College until he took his degree (1749.) He was again lowest in the list; but still he had passed; and he must have learned something.   He was now twenty-one, with all the world before him; and the question was as to how he was to employ such knowledge as he had acquired.

CHAPTER III.

But Goldsmith was not in any hurry to acquire either wealth or fame. He had a happy knack of enjoying the present hour—especially when there were one or two boon companions with him, and a pack of cards to be found; and, after his return to his mother's house, he appears to have entered upon the business of idleness with much philosophical satisfaction. If he was not quite such an unlettered clown as he has described in Tony Lumpkin, he had at least all Tony Lumpkin's high spirits and love of joking and idling; and he was surrounded at the ale-house by just such a company of admirers as used to meet at the famous Three Pigeons. Sometimes he helped in his brother's school; sometimes he went errands for his mother; occasionally he would sit and meditatively play the flute—for the day was to be passed somehow; then in the evening came the assemblage in Conway's inn, with the glass, and the pipe, and the cards, and the uproarious jest or song. "But Scripture saith an ending to all fine things must be," and the friends of this jovial young " buckeen " began to tire of his idleness and his recurrent visits. They gave him hints that he might set about doing something to provide himself with a living; and the first thing they thought of was that he should go into the Church—perhaps as a sort of purification-house after George Conway's inn. Accordingly Goldsmith, who appears to have been a most good-natured and compliant youth, did make application to the Bishop of Elphin. There is some doubt about the precise reasons which induced the Bishop to decline Goldsmith's application, but at any rate the Church, was denied the aid of the young man's eloquence and erudition. Then he tried teaching, and through the good offices of his uncle he obtained a tutorship which he held for a considerable time—long enough, indeed, to enable him to amass a sum of thirty pounds. When he quarrelled with his patron, and once more "took the world for his pillow," as the Gaelic stories say, he had this sum in his pocket and was possessed of a good horse.

He started away from Ballymahon, where his mother was now living, with some vague notion of making his fortune as casual circumstance might direct. The expedition came to a premature end; and he returned without the money, and on the back of a wretched animal, telling his mother a cock-and-bull story of the most amusing simplicity. " If Uncle Contarine believed those letters," says Mr. Thackeray, " —— if Oliver's mother believed that story which the youth related of his going to Cork, with the purpose of embarking for America ; of his having paid his passage-money, and having sent his kit on board ; of the anony-mous captain sailing away with Oliver's valuable luggage, in a nameless ship, never to return ; if Uncle Contarine and the mother at Ballymahon believed his stories, they must have been a very simple pair ; as it was a very simple rogue indeed who cheated them." Indeed, if any one is anxious to fill up this hiatus in Goldsmith's life, the best thing he can do is to discard Goldsmith's suspicious record of his adventures, and put in its place the faithful record of the adventures of Mr. Barry Lyndon, when that modest youth left his mother's house and rode to Dublin, with a certain number of guineas in his pocket. But whether Uncle Contarine believed the story or no, he was ready to give the young gentleman another chance ; and this time it was the legal profession that was chosen. Goldsmith got fifty pounds from his uncle, and reached Dublin. In a remarkably brief space of time he had gambled away the fifty pounds, and was on his way back to Ballymahon, where his mother's reception of him was not very cordial, though his uncle forgave him, and was once more ready to start him in life. But in what direction ? Teaching, the Church, and the law had lost their attractions for him. Well, this time it was medicine. In fact, any sort of project was capable of drawing forth the good old uncle's bounty. The funds were again forthcoming ; Goldsmith started for Edinburgh, and now (1752) saw Ireland for the last time.

He lived, and he informed his uncle that he studied, in Edinburgh for a year and a half ; at the end of which time it appeared to him that his knowledge of medicine would be much improved by foreign travel. There was Albinus, for example, "the great professor of Leyden," as he wrote to the credulous uncle, from

C

whom he would doubtless learn much. When, having got another twenty pounds for travelling expenses, he did reach Leyden (1754), he mentioned Gaubius, the chemical professor. Gaubius is also a good name. That his intercourse with these learned persons, and the serious nature of his studies, were not incompatible with a little light relaxation in the way of gambling is not impossible. On one occasion, it is said, he was so lucky that he came to a fellow-student with his pockets full of money; and was induced to resolve never to play again—a resolution broken about as soon as made. Of course he lost all his winnings, and more; and had to borrow a trifling sum to get himself out of the place. Then an incident occurs which is highly characteristic of the better side of Goldsmith's nature. He had just got this money, and was about to leave Leyden, when, as Mr. Forster writes, " he passed a florist's garden on his return, and seeing some rare and high-priced flower, which his uncle Contarine, an enthusiast in such things, had often spoken and been in search of, he ran in without other thought than of immediate pleasure to his kindest friend, bought a parcel of the roots, and sent them off to Ireland." He had a guinea in his pocket when he started on the grand tour.

Of this notable period in Goldsmith's life (1755–6) very little is known, though a good deal has been guessed. A minute record of all the personal adventures that befell the wayfarer as he trudged from country to country, a diary of the odd humours and fancies that must have occurred to him in his solitary pilgrimages, would be of quite inestimable value; but even the letters that Goldsmith wrote home from time to time are lost; while *The*

Traveller consists chiefly of a series of philosophical reflections on the government of various states, more likely to have engaged the attention of a Fleet-street author, living in an atmosphere of books, than to have occupied the mind of a tramp anxious about his supper and his night's lodging. Boswell says he "disputed" his way through Europe. It is much more probable that he begged his way through Europe. The romantic version, which has been made the subject of many a charming picture, is that he was entertained by the peasantry whom he had delighted with his playing on the flute. It is quite probable that Goldsmith, whose imagination had been captivated by the story of how Baron von Holberg had as a young man really passed through France, Germany, and Holland in this Orpheus-like manner, may have put a flute in his pocket when he left Leyden; but it is far from safe to assume, as is generally done, that Goldsmith was himself the hero of the adventures described in Chapter xx. of the *Vicar of Wakefield*. It is the more to be regretted that we have no authentic record of these devious wanderings, that by this time Goldsmith had acquired, as is shown in other letters, a polished, easy, and graceful style, with a very considerable faculty of humorous observation. Those ingenious letters to his uncle (they usually included a little hint about money) were, in fact, a trifle too literary both in substance and in form; we could even now, looking at them with a pardonable curiosity, have spared a little of their formal antithesis for some more precise information about the writer and his surroundings.

The strangest thing about this strange journey all over

Europe was the failure of Goldsmith to pick up even a
common and ordinary acquaintance with the familiar facts
of natural history. The ignorance on this point of the
author of the *Animated Nature* was a constant subject of
jest among Goldsmith's friends. They declared he could
not tell the difference between any two sorts of barndoor
fowl until he saw them cooked and on the table. But it
may be said prematurely here that, even when he is
wrong as to his facts or his sweeping generalisations,
one is inclined to forgive him on account of the quaint
gracefulness and point of his style. When Mr. Burchell
says, "This rule seems to extend even to other animals:
the little vermin race are ever treacherous, cruel, and
cowardly, whilst those endowed with strength and
power are generous, brave, and gentle," we scarcely
stop to reflect that the merlin, which is not much bigger
than a thrush, has an extraordinary courage and spirit,
while the lion, if all stories be true, is, unless when
goaded by hunger, an abject skulker. Elsewhere, indeed,
in the *Animated Nature*, Goldsmith gives credit to the
smaller birds for a good deal of valour, and then
goes on to say, with a charming freedom,—" But their
contentions are sometimes of a gentler nature. Two
male birds shall strive in song till, after a long
struggle, the loudest shall entirely silence the other.
During these contentions the female sits an attentive
silent auditor, and often rewards the loudest songster
with her company during the season." Yet even this
description of the battle of the bards, with the queen of
love as arbiter, is scarcely so amusing as his happy-
go-lucky notions with regard to the variability of
species. The philosopher, flute in hand, who went

wandering from the canals of Holland to the ice-ribbed
falls of the Rhine, may have heard from time to time
that contest between singing-birds which he so imagin-
atively describes; but it was clearly the Fleet-Street
author, living among books, who arrived at the conclusion that intermarriage of species is common among
small birds and rare among big birds. Quoting some
lines of Addison's which express the belief that birds
are a virtuous race—that the nightingale, for example,
does not covet the wife of his neighbour, the blackbird
—Goldsmith goes on to observe,—"But whatever may
be the poet's opinion, the probability is against this
fidelity among the smaller tenants of the grove. The
great birds are much more true to their species than
these; and, of consequence, the varieties among them
are more few. Of the ostrich, the cassowary, and the
eagle, there are but few species; and no arts that man
can use could probably induce them to mix with each
other."

What he did bring back from his foreign travels
was a medical degree. Where he got it, and how
he got it, are alike matters of pure conjecture; but
it is extremely improbable that—whatever he might
have been willing to write home from Padua or
Louvain, in order to coax another remittance from his
Irish friends—he would afterwards, in the presence of
such men as Johnson, Burke, and Reynolds, wear sham
honours. It is much more probable that, on his finding
those supplies from Ireland running ominously short,
the philosophic vagabond determined to prove to his
correspondents that he was really at work somewhere,
instead of merely idling away his time, begging or

borrowing the wherewithal to pass him from town to town. That he did see something of the foreign universities is evident from his own writings ; there are touches of description here and there which he could not well have got from books. With this degree, and with such book-learning and such knowledge of nature and human nature as he had chosen or managed to pick up during all those years, he was now called upon to begin life for himself. The Irish supplies stopped altogether. His letters were left unanswered. And so Goldsmith somehow or other got back to London (February 1, 1756), and had to cast about for some way of earning his daily bread.

CHAPTER IV.

HERE ensued a very dark period in his life. He was
alone in London, without friends, without money, without introductions ; his appearance was the reverse of pre-
possessing ; and, even despite that medical degree and
his acquaintance with the learned Albinus and the
learned Gaubius, he had practically nothing of any
value to offer for sale in the great labour-market of the
world. How he managed to live at all is a mystery : it
is certain that he must have endured a great deal of
want ; and one may well sympathise with so gentle and
sensitive a creature reduced to such straits, without in-
quiring too curiously into the causes of his misfortunes.
If, on the one hand, we cannot accuse society, or
Christianity, or the English government of injustice and
cruelty because Goldsmith had gambled away his chances
and was now called on to pay the penalty, on the other
hand, we had better, before blaming Goldsmith himself,
inquire into the origin of those defects of character which
produced such results. As this would involve an *excur-
sus* into the controversy between Necessity and Free-will,
probably most people would rather leave it alone. It may

safely be said in any case that, while Goldsmith's faults
and follies, of which he himself had to suffer the consequences, are patent enough, his character on the whole
was distinctly a lovable one. Goldsmith was his own
enemy, and everybody else's friend : that is not a
serious indictment, as things go. He was quite well
aware of his weaknesses ; and he was also—it may be
hinted—aware of the good-nature which he put forward
as condonation. If some foreigner were to ask how it
is that so thoroughly a commercial people as the English
are—strict in the acknowledgment and payment of debt
—should have always betrayed a sneaking fondness for
the character of the good-humoured scapegrace whose
hand is in everybody's pocket, and who throws away other
people's money with the most charming air in the world,
Goldsmith might be pointed to as one of many literary
teachers whose own circumstances were not likely to
make them severe censors of the Charles Surfaces, or
lenient judges of the Joseph Surfaces of the world.
Be merry while you may ; let to-morrow take care
of itself ; share your last guinea with any one, even
if the poor drones of society—the butcher, and baker,
and milkman with his score—have to suffer ; do anything you like, so long as you keep the heart warm.
All this is a delightful philosophy. It has its moments
of misery—its periods of reaction—but it has its
moments of high delight. When we are invited to
contemplate the "evil destinies of men of letters,"
we ought to be shown the flood-tides as well as the
ebb-tides. The tavern gaiety ; the brand new coat
and lace and sword ; the midnight frolics, with jolly
companions every one—these, however brief and inter-

mittent, should not be wholly left out of the picture. Of course it is very dreadful to hear of poor Boyse lying in bed with nothing but a blanket over him, and with his arms thrust through two holes in the blanket, so that he could write—perhaps a continuation of his poem on the *Deity*. But then we should be shown Boyse when he was spending the money collected by Dr. Johnson to get the poor scribbler's clothes out of pawn ; and we should also be shown him, with his hands through the holes in the blanket, enjoying the mushrooms and truffles on which, as a little garniture for " his last scrap of beef," he had just laid out his last half-guinea.

There were but few truffles—probably there was but little beef—for Goldsmith during this sombre period. " His threadbare coat, his uncouth figure, and Hibernian dialect caused him to meet with repeated refusals." But at length he got some employment in a chemist's shop, and this was a start. Then he tried practising in a small way on his own account in Southwark. Here he made the acquaintance of a printer's workman ; and through him he was engaged as corrector of the press in the establishment of Mr. Samuel Richardson. Being so near to literature, he caught the infection ; and naturally began with a tragedy. This tragedy was shown to the author of *Clarissa Harlowe ;* but it only went the way of many similar first inspiritings of the Muse. Then Goldsmith drifted to Peckham, where we find him (1757) installed as usher at Dr. Milner's school. Goldsmith as usher has been the object of much sympathy ; and he would certainly deserve it, if we are to assume that his description of an usher's position in the *Bee*, and in George Primrose's advice to his cousin, was a full and

accurate description of his life at Peckham. "Browbeat
by the master, hated for my ugly face by the mistress,
worried by the boys "—if that was his life, he was much
to be pitied. But we cannot believe it. The Milners
were exceedingly kind to Goldsmith. It was at the
intercession of young Milner, who had been his fellow-
student at Edinburgh, that Goldsmith got the situation,
which at all events kept him out of the reach of immediate want. It was through the Milners that he
was introduced to Griffiths, who gave him a chance of
trying a literary career—as a hack-writer of reviews and
so forth. When, having got tired of that, Goldsmith
was again floating vaguely on the waves of chance,
where did he find a harbour but in that very school at
Peckham? And we have the direct testimony of the
youngest of Dr. Milner's daughters, that this Irish
usher of theirs was a remarkably cheerful, and even
facetious person, constantly playing tricks and practical
jokes, amusing the boys by telling stories and by performances on the flute, living a careless life, and
always in advance of his salary. Any beggars, or group
of children, even the very boys who played back practical
jokes on him, were welcome to a share of what small
funds he had; and we all know how Mrs. Milner good-
naturedly said one day, "You had better, Mr. Goldsmith, let me keep your money for you, as I do for some
of the young gentlemen;" and how he answered with
much simplicity, "In truth, Madam, there is equal
need." With Goldsmith's love of approbation and
extreme sensitiveness he no doubt suffered deeply from
many slights, now as at other times; but what we know
of his life in the Peckham school does not incline us to

believe that it was an especially miserable period of his existence. His abundant cheerfulness does not seem to have at any time deserted him ; and what with tricks, and jokes, and playing of the flute, the dull routine of instructing the unruly young gentlemen at Dr. Milner's was got through somehow.

When Goldsmith left the Peckham school to try hack-writing in Paternoster Row, he was going further to fare worse. Griffiths the bookseller, when he met Goldsmith at Dr. Milner's dinner-table and invited him to become a reviewer, was doing a service to the English nation—for it was in this period of machine-work that Goldsmith discovered that happy faculty of literary expression that led to the composition of his masterpieces— but he was doing little immediate service to Goldsmith.

The newly-captured hack was boarded and lodged at Griffiths' house in Paternoster Row (1757); he was to have a small salary in consideration of remorselessly constant work ; and—what was the hardest condition of all—he was to have his writings revised by Mrs. Griffiths. Mr. Forster justly remarks that though at last Goldsmith had thus become a man-of-letters, he "had gratified no passion and attained no object of ambition." He had taken to literature, as so many others have done, merely as a last resource. And if it is true that literature at first treated Goldsmith harshly, made him work hard, and gave him comparatively little for what he did, at least it must be said that his experience was not a singular one. Mr. Forster says that literature was at that time in a transition state : "The patron was gone, and the public had not come." But when Goldsmith began to do better than hack-work, he found a public

speedily enough.   If, as Lord Macaulay computes, Goldsmith received in the last seven years of his life what
was equivalent to £5,600 of our money, even the villain
booksellers cannot be accused of having starved him.
At the outset of his literary career he received no large
sums, for he had achieved no reputation; but he got
the market-rate for his work.   We have around us at this
moment plenty of hacks who do not earn much more
than their board and lodging with a small salary.

For the rest, we have no means of knowing whether
Goldsmith got through his work with ease or with diffi-
culty; but it is obvious, looking over the reviews which
he is believed to have written for Griffiths' magazine,
that he readily acquired the professional critic's airs
of superiority, along with a few tricks of the trade, no
doubt taught him by Griffiths.   Several of these reviews,
for example, are merely epitomes of the contents of the
books reviewed, with some vague suggestion that the
writer might, if he had been less careful, have done
worse, and, if he had been more careful, might have
done better.   Who does not remember how the philosophic vagabond was taught to become a cognoscento?
"The whole secret consisted in a strict adherence to
two rules: the one always to observe that the picture
might have been better if the painter had taken more
pains; and the other to praise the works of Pietro
Perugino."   It is amusing to observe the different
estimates formed of the function of criticism by Goldsmith the critic, and by Goldsmith the author.   Goldsmith, sitting at Griffiths' desk, naturally magnifies his
office, and announces his opinion that "to direct our
taste, and conduct the poet up to perfection, has ever

been the true critic's province." But Goldsmith the author, when he comes to inquire into the existing state of Polite Learning in Europe, finds in criticism not a help but a danger. It is "the natural destroyer of polite learning." And again, in the *Citizen of the World*, he exclaims against the pretensions of the critic. "If any choose to be critics, it is but saying they are critics; and from that time forward they become invested with full power and authority over every caitiff who aims at their instruction or entertainment."

This at least may be said, that in these early essays contributed to the *Monthly Review* there is much more of Goldsmith the critic than of Goldsmith the author. They are somewhat laboured performances. They are almost devoid of the sly and delicate humour that afterwards marked Goldsmith's best prose work. We find throughout his trick of antithesis; but here it is forced and formal, whereas afterwards he lent to this habit of writing the subtle surprise of epigram. They have the true manner of authority, nevertheless. He says of Home's *Douglas*—"Those parts of nature, and that rural simplicity with which the author was, perhaps, best acquainted, are not unhappily described; and hence we are led to conjecture, that a more universal knowledge of nature will probably increase his powers of description." If the author had written otherwise, he would have written differently; had he known more, he would not have been so ignorant; the tragedy is a tragedy, but why did not the author make it a comedy?—this sort of criticism has been heard of even in our own day. However, Goldsmith pounded away at his newly-found work, under the eye of the exacting book-

seller and his learned wife. We find him dealing with
Scandinavian (here called Celtic) mythology, though he
does not adventure on much comment of his own ; then
he engages Smollett's *History of England*, but mostly in
the way of extract ; anon we find him reviewing *A Journal
of Eight Days' Journey*, by Jonas Hanway, of whom
Johnson said that he made some reputation by travelling
abroad, and lost it all by travelling at home. Then again
we find him writing a disquisition on *Some Enquiries
concerning the First Inhabitants, Language, Religion,
Learning, and Letters of Europe*, by a Mr. Wise, who,
along with his critic, appears to have got into hopeless
confusion in believing Basque and Armorican to be the
remains of the same ancient language. The last phrase
of a note appended to this review by Goldsmith probably
indicates his own humble estimate of his work at this
time. " It is more our business," he says, " to exhibit
the opinions of the learned than to controvert them."
In fact he was employed to boil down books for
people who did not wish to spend more on literature
than the price of a magazine. Though he was new to
the trade, it is probable he did it as well as any other.

At the end of five months, Goldsmith and Griffiths
quarrelled and separated. Griffiths said Goldsmith was
idle ; Goldsmith said Griffiths was impertinent ; probably
the editorial supervision exercised by Mrs. Griffiths had
something to do with the dire contention. From Paternoster Row Goldsmith removed to a garret in Fleet
Street ; had his letters addressed to a coffee-house ; and
apparently supported himself by further hack-work, his
connection with Griffiths not being quite severed. Then
he drifted back to Peckham again ; and was once more

installed as usher, Dr. Milner being in especial want of
an assistant at this time. Goldsmith's lingering about
the gates of literature had not inspired him with any
great ambition to enter the enchanted land. But at the
same time he thought he saw in literature a means by
which a little ready money might be made, in order to
help him on to something more definite and substantial ;
and this goal was now put before him by Dr. Milner, in
the shape of a medical appointment on the Coromandel
coast. It was in the hope of obtaining this appointment,
that he set about composing that *Enquiry into the
Present State of Polite Learning in Europe*, which is now
interesting to us as the first of his more ambitious works.
As the book grew under his hands, he began to cast
about for subscribers ; and from the Fleet-Street coffee-
house—he had again left the Peckham school—he
addressed to his friends and relatives a series of letters
of the most charming humour, which might have drawn
subscriptions from a millstone. To his brother-in-law,
Mr. Hodson, he sent a glowing account of the great
fortune in store for him on the Coromandel coast. "The
salary is but trifling," he writes, "namely £100 per
annum, but the other advantages, if a person be prudent,
are considerable. The practice of the place, if I am
rightly informed, generally amounts to not less than
£1,000 per annum, for which the appointed physician
has an exclusive privilege. This, with the advantages
resulting from trade, and the high interest which money
bears, viz. £20 per cent., are the inducements which
persuade me to undergo the fatigues of sea, the dangers
of war, and the still greater dangers of the climate ;
which induce me to leave a place where I am every day

gaining friends and esteem, and where I might enjoy all
the conveniences of life."

The surprising part of this episode in Goldsmith's
life is that he did really receive the appointment ; in
fact he was called upon to pay £10 for the appoint-
ment-warrant. In this emergency he went to the
proprietor of the *Critical Review*, the rival of the
Monthly, and obtained some money for certain anonymous work which need not be mentioned in detail
here. He also moved into another garret, this time
in Green-Arbour Court, Fleet Street, in a wilderness
of slums. The Coromandel project, however, on which
so many hopes had been built, fell through. No ex-
planation of the collapse could be got from either Goldsmith himself, or from Dr. Milner. Mr. Forster suggests
that Goldsmith's inability to raise money for his outfit
may have been made the excuse for transferring the
appointment to another ; and that is probable enough ;
but it is also probable that the need for such an excuse
was based on the discovery that Goldsmith was not
properly qualified for the post. And this seems the more
likely, that Goldsmith immediately afterwards resolved
to challenge examination at Surgeons' Hall. He undertook to write four articles for the *Monthly Review ;*
Griffiths became surety to a tailor for a fine suit of
clothes ; and thus equipped, Goldsmith presented himself at Surgeons' Hall. He only wanted to be passed as
hospital mate ; but even that modest ambition was un-
fulfilled. He was found not qualified ; and returned,
with his fine clothes, to his Fleet-Street den. He was
now thirty years of age (1758) ; and had found no definite
occupation in the world.

CHAPTER V.

DURING the period that now ensued, and amid much quarrelling with Griffiths and hack-writing for the *Critical Review,* Goldsmith managed to get his *Enquiry into the Present State of Polite Learning in Europe* completed ; and it is from the publication of that work, on the 2nd of April, 1759, that we may date the beginning of Goldsmith's career as an author. The book was published anonymously; but Goldsmith was not at all anxious to disclaim the parentage of his first-born ; and in Grub Street and its environs, at least, the authorship of the book was no secret. Moreover there was that in it which was likely to provoke the literary tribe to plenty of fierce talking. The *Enquiry* is neither more nor less than an endeavour to prove that criticism has in all ages been the deadly enemy of art and literature ; coupled with an appeal to authors to draw their inspiration from nature rather than from books, and varied here and there by a gentle sigh over the loss of that patronage, in the sunshine of which men of genius were wont to bask. Goldsmith, not having been an author himself, could not have suffered much at the

D

hands of the critics ; so that it is not to be supposed that
personal feeling dictated this fierce onslaught on the
whole tribe of critics, compilers, and commentators.
They are represented to us as rank weeds, growing up
to choke all manifestations of true art. "Ancient
learning," we are told at the outset, "may be distinguished into three periods : its commencement, or
the age of poets ; its maturity, or the age of philo-
sophers ; and its decline, or the age of critics." Then
our guide carries us into the dark ages ; and, with
lantern in hand, shows us the creatures swarming
there in the sluggish pools—"commentators, compilers,
polemic divines, and intricate metaphysicians." We
come to Italy : look at the affectations with which the
Virtuosi and Filosofi have enchained the free spirit of
poetry. " Poetry is no longer among them an imitation
of what we see, but of what a visionary might wish.
The zephyr breathes the most exquisite perfume ; the
trees wear eternal verdure ; fawns, and dryads, and
hamadryads, stand ready to fan the sultry shepherdess,
who has forgot, indeed, the prettiness with which
Guarini's shepherdesses have been reproached, but is
so simple and innocent as often to have no meaning.
Happy country, where the pastoral age begins to re-
vive !—where the wits even of Rome are united into a
rural group of nymphs and swains, under the appellation
of modern Arcadians !—where in the midst of porticoes,
processions, and cavalcades, abbés turned shepherds
and shepherdesses without sheep indulge their innocent
divertimenti ! "

In Germany the ponderous volumes of the commentators next come in for animadversion ; and here we

find an epigram, the quaint simplicity of which is peculiarly characteristic of Goldsmith. "Were angels to write books," he remarks, "they never would write folios." But Germany gets credit for the money spent by her potentates on learned institutions; and it is perhaps England that is delicately hinted at in these words : "Had the fourth part of the immense sum above-mentioned been given in proper rewards to genius, in some neighbouring countries, it would have rendered the name of the donor immortal, and added to the real interests of society." Indeed, when we come to England, we find that men of letters are in a bad way, owing to the prevalence of critics, the tyranny of booksellers, and the absence of patrons. "The author, when unpatronized by the great, has naturally recourse to the bookseller. There cannot perhaps be imagined a combination more prejudicial to taste than this. It is the interest of the one to allow as little for writing, and of the other to write as much as possible. Accordingly, tedious compilations and periodical magazines are the result of their joint endeavours. In these circumstances the author bids adieu to fame, writes for bread, and for that only. Imagination is seldom called in. He sits down to address the venal muse with the most phlegmatic apathy; and, as we are told of the Russian, courts his mistress by falling asleep in her lap. His reputation never spreads in a wider circle than that of the trade, who generally value him, not for the fineness of his compositions, but the quantity he works off in a given time.

"A long habit of writing for bread thus turns the

ambition of every author at last into avarice. He finds
that he has written many years, that the public are
scarcely acquainted even with his name ; he despairs of
applause, and turns to profit, which invites him. He
finds that money procures all those advantages, that
respect, and that ease which he vainly expected from
fame. Thus the man who, under the protection of the
great, might have done honour to humanity, when only
patronized by the bookseller, becomes a thing little
superior to the fellow who works at the press."

Nor was he afraid to attack the critics of his own
day, though he knew that the two Reviews for which he
had recently been writing would have something to say
about his own *Enquiry*. This is how he disposes of
the *Critical* and the *Monthly* : " We have two literary
Reviews in London, with critical newspapers and magazines without number. The compilers of these resemble
the commoners of Rome ; they are all for levelling
property, not by increasing their own, but by diminish-
ing that of others. The man who has any good-
nature in his disposition must, however, be somewhat
displeased to see distinguished reputations often the
sport of ignorance,—to see, by one false pleasantry,
the future peace of a worthy man's life disturbed, and
this only because he has unsuccessfully attempted to
instruct or amuse us. Though ill-nature is far from
being wit, yet it is generally laughed at as such. The
critic enjoys the triumph, and ascribes to his parts what
is only due to his effrontery. I fire with indignation,
when I see persons wholly destitute of education and
genius indent to the press, and thus turn book-makers,
adding to the sin of criticism the sin of ignorance also ;

whose trade is a bad one, and who are bad workmen in the trade." Indeed there was a good deal of random hitting in the *Enquiry*, which was sure to provoke resentment. Why, for example, should he have gone out of his way to insult the highly respectable class of people who excel in mathematical studies ? "This seems a science," he observes, "to which the meanest intellects are equal. I forget who it is that says 'All men might understand mathematics if they would.'" There was also in the first edition of the *Enquiry* a somewhat ungenerous attack on stage-managers, actors, actresses, and theatrical things in general ; but this was afterwards wisely excised. It is not to be wondered at that, on the whole, the *Enquiry* should have been severely handled in certain quarters. Smollett, who reviewed it in the *Critical Review*, appears to have kept his temper pretty well for a Scotchman ; but Kenrick, a hack employed by Griffiths to maltreat the book in the *Monthly Review*, flourished his bludgeon in a brave manner. The coarse personalities and malevolent insinuations of this bully no doubt hurt Goldsmith considerably ; but, as we look at them now, they are only remarkable for their dulness. If Griffiths had had another Goldsmith to reply to Goldsmith, the retort would have been better worth reading : one can imagine the playful sarcasm that would have been dealt out to this new writer, who, in the very act of protesting against criticism, proclaimed himself a critic. But Goldsmiths are not always to be had when wanted ; while Kenricks can be bought at any moment for a guinea or two a head.

Goldsmith had not chosen literature as the occupation

of his life; he had only fallen back on it, when other projects failed. But it is quite possible that now, as he began to take up some slight position as an author, the old ambition of distinguishing himself—which had flickered before his imagination from time to time—began to enter into his calculations along with the more pressing business of earning a livelihood. And he was soon to have an opportunity of appealing to a wider public than could have been expected for that erudite treatise on the arts of Europe. Mr. Wilkie, a book-seller in St. Paul's Churchyard, proposed to start a weekly magazine, price threepence, to contain essays, short stories, letters on the topics of the day, and so forth, more or less after the manner of the *Spectator*. He asked Goldsmith to become sole contributor. Here, indeed, was a very good opening; for, although there were many magazines in the field, the public had just then a fancy for literature in small doses; while Gold-smith, in entering into the competition, would not be hampered by the dulness of collaborateurs. He closed with Wilkie's offer; and on the 6th of October, 1759, appeared the first number of the *Bee*.

For us now there is a curious autobiographical interest in the opening sentences of the first number; but surely even the public of the day must have imagined that the new writer who was now addressing them, was not to be confounded with the common herd of magazine-hacks. What could be more delightful than this odd mixture of modesty, humour, and an anxious desire to please?— "There is not, perhaps, a more whimsically dismal figure in nature than a man of real modesty, who assumes an air of impudence—who, while his heart beats with anxiety, studies ease and affects good-humour.   In this situation, however, a periodical writer often finds himself upon his first attempt to address the public in form. All his power of pleasing is damped by solicitude, and his cheerfulness dashed with apprehension. Impressed with the terrors of the tribunal before which he is going to appear, his natural humour turns to pertness, and for real wit he is obliged to substitute vivacity. His first publication draws a crowd ; they part dissatisfied ; and the author, never more to be indulged with a favourable hearing, is left to condemn the indelicacy of his own address or their want of discernment. For my part, as I was never distinguished for address, and have often even blundered in making my bow, such bodings as these had like to have totally repressed my ambition.   I was at a loss whether to give the public specious promises, or give none ; whether to be merry or sad on this solemn occasion.   If I should decline all merit, it was too probable the hasty reader might have taken me at my word.   If, on the other hand, like labourers in the magazine trade, I had, with modest impudence, humbly presumed to promise an epitome of all the good things that ever were said or written, this might have disgusted those readers I most desire to please. Had I been merry, I might have been censured as vastly low ; and had I been sorrowful, I might have been left to mourn in solitude and silence ; in short, whichever way I turned, nothing presented but prospects of terror, despair, chandlers' shops, and waste paper."

And it is just possible that if Goldsmith had kept to this vein of familiar *causerie*, the public might in time have been attracted by its quaintness.   But no doubt

Mr. Wilkie would have stared aghast; and so we find
Goldsmith, as soon as his introductory bow is made,
setting seriously about the business of magazine-making.
Very soon, however, both Mr. Wilkie and his editor
perceived that the public had not been taken by their
venture. The chief cause of the failure, as it appears
to any one who looks over the magazine now, would
seem to be the lack of any definite purpose. There was
no marked feature to arrest public attention, while
many things were discarded on which the popularity
of other periodicals had been based. There was no
scandal to appeal to the key-hole and back-door
element in human nature; there were no libels and
gross personalities to delight the mean and envious;
there were no fine airs of fashion to charm milliners
anxious to know how the great talked, and posed, and
dressed; and there was no solemn and pompous erudition to impress the minds of those serious and sensible
people who buy literature as they buy butter, by its
weight. At the beginning of No. IV. he admits that
the new magazine has not been a success; and, in doing
so, returns to that vein of whimsical, personal humour
with which he had started : " Were I to measure the
merit of my present undertaking by its success or the
rapidity of its sale, I might be led to form conclusions
by no means favourable to the pride of an author.
Should I estimate my fame by its extent, every newspaper and magazine would leave me far behind. Their
fame is diffused in a very wide circle—that of some as
far as Islington, and some yet farther still; while mine,
I sincerely believe, has hardly travelled beyond the
sound of Bow Bell ; and, while the works of others fly

like unpinioned swans, I find my own move as heavily
as a new-plucked goose.   Still, however, I have as much
pride as they who have ten times as many readers.   It
is impossible to repeat all the agreeable delusions in
which a disappointed author is apt to find comfort.   I
conclude, that what my reputation wants in extent is
made up by its solidity.   *Minus juvat gloria lata quam
magna.*   I have great satisfaction in considering the
delicacy and discernment of those readers I have, and in
ascribing my want of popularity to the ignorance or
inattention of those I have not.   All the world may
forsake an author, but vanity will never forsake him.
Yet, notwithstanding so sincere a confession, I was once
induced to show my indignation against the public, by
discontinuing my endeavours to please ; and was bravely
resolved, like Raleigh, to vex them by burning my manuscript in a passion.   Upon recollection, however, I considered what set or body of people would be displeased
at my rashness.   The sun, after so sad an accident,
might shine next morning as bright as usual ; men
might laugh and sing the next day, and transact business as before, and not a single creature feel any regret
but myself.''

Goldsmith was certainly more at home in this sort of
writing, than in gravely lecturing people against the
vice of gambling ; in warning tradesmen how ill it
became them to be seen at races ; in demonstrating
that justice is a higher virtue than generosity ; and
in proving that the avaricious are the true bene-
factors of society.   But even as he confesses the failure
of his new magazine, he seems determined to show the
public what sort of writer this is, whom as yet they have

not regarded too favourably. It is in No. IV. of the *Bee* that the famous *City Night Piece* occurs. No doubt that strange little fragment of description was the result of some sudden and aimless fancy, striking the occupant of the lonely garret in the middle of the night. The present tense, which he seldom used—and the abuse of which is one of the detestable vices of modern literature—adds to the mysterious solemnity of the recital :—

" The clock has just struck two, the expiring taper rises and sinks in the socket, the watchman forgets the hour in slumber, the laborious and the happy are at rest, and nothing wakes but meditation, guilt, revelry, and despair. The drunkard once more fills the destroying bowl, the robber walks his midnight round, and the suicide lifts his guilty arm against his own sacred person.

" Let me no longer waste the night over the page of antiquity or the sallies of contemporary genius, but pursue the solitary walk, where Vanity, ever changing, but a few hours past walked before me—where she kept up the pageant, and now, like a froward child, seems hushed with her own importunities.

" What a gloom hangs all around ! The dying lamp feebly emits a yellow gleam ; no sound is heard but of the chiming clock, or the distant watch-dog. All the bustle of human pride is forgotten ; an hour like this may well display the emptiness of human vanity.

" There will come a time, when this temporary solitude may be made continual, and the city itself, like its inhabitants, fade away, and leave a desert in its room.

" What cities, as great as this, have once triumphed in

existence, had their victories as great, joy as just and as unbounded; and, with short-sighted presumption, promised themselves immortality! Posterity can hardly trace the situation of some; the sorrowful traveller wanders over the awful ruins of others; and, as he beholds, he learns wisdom, and feels the transience of every sublunary possession.

" ' Here,' he cries, ' stood their citadel, now grown over with weeds; there their senate-house, but now the haunt of every noxious reptile; temples and theatres stood here, now only an undistinguished heap of ruin. They are fallen, for luxury and avarice first made them feeble. The rewards of the state were conferred on amusing, and not on useful, members of society. Their riches and opulence invited the invaders, who, though at first repulsed, returned again, conquered by perseverance, and at last swept the defendants into undistinguished destruction.' "

CHAPTER VI.

PERSONAL TRAITS.

THE foregoing extracts will sufficiently show what were the chief characteristics of Goldsmith's writing at this time—the grace and ease of style, a gentle and sometimes pathetic thoughtfulness, and, above all, when he speaks in the first person, a delightful vein of humorous self-disclosure. Moreover, these qualities, if they were not immediately profitable to the booksellers, were beginning to gain for him the recognition of some of the well-known men of the day. Percy, afterwards Bishop of Dromore, had made his way to the miserable garret of the poor author. Smollett, whose novels Goldsmith preferred to his History, was anxious to secure his services as a contributor to the forthcoming *British Magazine*. Burke had spoken of the pleasure given him by Goldsmith's review of the *Enquiry into the Origin of our Ideas of the Sublime and Beautiful*. But, to crown all, the great Cham himself sought out this obscure author, who had on several occasions spoken with reverence and admiration of his works; and so began what is perhaps the most interesting literary friendship on record. At what precise date Johnson first made Goldsmith's acquaintance, is not

known; Mr. Forster is right in assuming that they
had met before the supper in Wine-Office Court, at
which Mr. Percy was present. It is a thousand pities
that Boswell had not by this time made his appearance
in London. Johnson, Goldsmith, and all the rest of
them are only ghosts until the pertinacious young laird
of Auchinleck comes on the scene to give them colour,
and life, and form. It is odd enough that the very first
remarks of Goldsmith's which Boswell jotted down in
his notebook, should refer to Johnson's systematic
kindness towards the poor and wretched. "He had
increased my admiration of the goodness of Johnson's
heart by incidental remarks in the course of conversation, such as, when I mentioned Mr. Levett, whom
he entertained under his roof, 'He is poor and honest,
which is recommendation enough to Johnson'; and
when I wondered that he was very kind to a man of
whom I had heard a very bad character, 'He is now
become miserable, and that ensures the protection of
Johnson.'"

For the rest, Boswell was not well-disposed towards
Goldsmith, whom he regarded with a jealousy equal to
his admiration of Johnson; but it is probable that his
description of the personal appearance of the awkward
and ungainly Irishman is in the main correct. And
here also it may be said that Boswell's love of truth
and accuracy compelled him to make this admission:
"It has been generally circulated and believed that he
(Goldsmith) was a mere fool in conversation; but, in
truth, this has been greatly exaggerated." On this exaggeration—seeing that the contributor to the *British
Magazine* and the *Public Ledger* was now becoming better

known among his fellow authors—a word or two may
fitly be said here. It pleased Goldsmith's contemporaries, who were not all of them celebrated for their
ready wit, to regard him as a hopeless and incurable
fool, who by some strange chance could produce literature, the merits of which he could not himself understand. To Horace Walpole we owe the phrase which
describes Goldsmith as an "inspired idiot." Innumer-
able stories are told of Goldsmith's blunders; of his
forced attempts to shine in conversation; of poor Poll
talking nonsense, when all the world was wondering
at the beauty of his writing. In one case we are told he
was content to admit, when dictated to, that this, and
not that, was what he really had meant in a particular
phrase. Now there can be no question that Goldsmith, conscious of his pitted face, his brogue, and his
ungainly figure, was exceedingly nervous and sensitive
in society, and was anxious, as such people mostly are,
to cover his shyness by an appearance of ease, if
not even of swagger; and there can be as little question
that he occasionally did and said very awkward and
blundering things. But our Japanese friend, whom we
mentioned in our opening pages, looking through the
record that is preserved to us of those blunders
which are supposed to be most conclusive as to
this aspect of Goldsmith's character, would certainly
stare. "Good heavens," he would cry, "did men ever
live who were so thick-headed as not to see the humour
of this or that 'blunder'; or were they so beset with
the notion that Goldsmith was only a fool, that they
must needs be blind?" Take one well-known instance.
He goes to France with Mrs. Horneck and her two

daughters, the latter very handsome young ladies. At
Lille the two girls and Goldsmith are standing at
the window of the hotel, overlooking the square in
which are some soldiers; and naturally the beautiful
young Englishwomen attract some attention. Thereupon Goldsmith turns indignantly away, remarking that
elsewhere he also has his admirers. Now what surgical
instrument was needed to get this harmless little joke
into any sane person's head? Boswell may perhaps be
pardoned for pretending to take the incident *au sérieux;*
for as has just been said, in his profound adoration of
Johnson, he was devoured by jealousy of Goldsmith;
but that any other mortal should have failed to see
what was meant by this little bit of humorous flattery
is almost incredible. No wonder that one of the sisters
afterwards referring to this "playful jest," should have
expressed her astonishment at finding it put down as a
proof of Goldsmith's envious disposition. But even after
that disclaimer, we find Mr. Croker, as quoted by Mr.
Forster, solemnly doubting "whether the vexation so
seriously exhibited by Goldsmith was real or assumed"!

Of course this is an extreme case; but there are others
very similar. "He affected," says Hawkins, "Johnson's
style and manner of conversation, and, when he had
uttered, as he often would, a laboured sentence, so
tumid as to be scarce intelligible, would ask if that was
not truly Johnsonian?" Is it not truly dismal to find
such an utterance coming from a presumably reasonable
human being? It is not to be wondered at that Goldsmith grew shy—and in some cases had to ward off the
acquaintance of certain of his neighbours as being too
intrusive—if he ran the risk of having his odd and grave

humours so densely mistranslated. The fact is this,
that Goldsmith was possessed of a very subtle quality
of humour, which is at all times rare, but which is
perhaps more frequently to be found in Irishmen
than among other folks. It consists in the satire of the
pretence and pomposities of others by means of a sort
of exaggerated and playful self-depreciation. It is a
most delicate and most delightful form of humour ; but
it is very apt to be misconstrued by the dull. Who
can doubt that Goldsmith was good-naturedly laughing at himself, his own plain face, his vanity, and
his blunders, when he professed to be jealous of the
admiration excited by the Miss Hornecks ; when he
gravely drew attention to the splendid colours of his
coat ; or when he no less gravely informed a company of
his friends that he had heard a very good story, but
would not repeat it, because they would be sure to miss
the point of it ?

This vein of playful and sarcastic self-depreciation is
continually cropping up in his essay writing, as, for
example, in the passage already quoted from No. IV.
of the *Bee*: "I conclude, that what my reputation
wants in extent, is made up by its solidity. *Minus
juvat gloria lata quam magna.* I have great satisfaction in considering the delicacy and discernment
of those readers I have, and in ascribing my want of
popularity to the ignorance or inattention of those I
have not." But here, no doubt, he remembers that he
is addressing the world at large, which contains many
foolish persons ; and so, that the delicate raillery may
not be mistaken, he immediately adds, "All the world
may forsake an author, but vanity will never forsake

him." That he expected a quicker apprehension on the part of his intimates and acquaintances, and that he was frequently disappointed, seems pretty clear from those very stories of his "blunders." We may reasonably suspect, at all events, that Goldsmith was not quite so much of a fool as he looked ; and it is far from improbable that when the ungainly Irishman was called in to make sport for the Philistines—and there were a good many Philistines in those days, if all stories be true— and when they imagined they had put him out of countenance, he was really standing aghast, and wondering how it could have pleased Providence to create such helpless stupidity.

E

CHAPTER VII.

THE CITIZEN OF THE WORLD.—BEAU NASH.

MEANWHILE, to return to his literary work, the *Citizen of the World* had grown out of his contributions to the *Public Ledger*, a daily newspaper started by Mr. Newbery, another bookseller in St. Paul's Churchyard. Goldsmith was engaged to write for this paper two letters a week at a guinea a-piece; and these letters were, after a short time (1760), written in the character of a Chinese who had come to study European civilisation. It may be noted that Goldsmith had in the *Monthly Review*, in mentioning Voltaire's memoirs of French writers, quoted a passage about Montesquieu's *Lettres Persanes* as follows: "It is written in imitation of the *Siamese Letters* of Du Freny and of the *Turkish Spy*; but it is an imitation which shows what the originals should have been. The success their works met with was, for the most part, owing to the foreign air of their performances; the success of the *Persian Letters* arose from the delicacy of their satire. That satire which in the mouth of an Asiatic is poignant, would lose all its force when coming from an European." And it must certainly be said that the charm of the strictures of the *Citizen of the World* lies wholly in their delicate satire, and not at all in any foreign air which the author may have tried to lend to these perform- ances. The disguise is very apparent. In those gar- rulous, vivacious, whimsical, and sometimes serious papers, Lien Chi Altangi, writing to Fum Hoam in Pekin, does not so much describe the aspects of European civilisation which would naturally surprise a Chinese, as he expresses the dissatisfaction of a European with certain phases of the civilisation visible everywhere around him. It is not a Chinaman, but a Fleet-Street author by profession, who resents the competition of noble amateurs whose works—otherwise bitter pills enough—are gilded by their titles :—" A nobleman has but to take a pen, ink, and paper, write away through three large volumes, and then sign his name to the title- page ; though the whole might have been before more disgusting than his own rent-roll, yet signing his name and title gives value to the deed, title being alone equi- valent to taste, imagination, and genius. As soon as a piece, therefore, is published, the first questions are— Who is the author ? Does he keep a coach ? Where lies his estate ? What sort of a table does he keep ? If he happens to be poor and unqualified for such a scrutiny, he and his works sink into irremediable obscurity, and too late he finds, that having fed upon turtle is a more ready way to fame than having digested Tully. The poor devil against whom fashion has set its face vainly alleges that he has been bred in every part of Europe where knowledge was to be sold ; that he has grown pale in the study of nature and himself. His works may please upon the perusal, but his pretensions

E 2

to fame are entirely disregarded. He is treated like a
fiddler, whose music, though liked, is not much praised,
because he lives by it; while a gentleman performer,
though the most wretched scraper alive, throws the
audience into raptures. The fiddler, indeed, may in
such a case console himself by thinking, that while the
other goes off with all the praise, he runs away with all
the money. But here the parallel drops; for while the
nobleman triumphs in unmerited applause, the author
by profession steals off with—nothing."

At the same time it must be allowed that the utterance
of these strictures through the mouth of a Chinese admits
of a certain *naïveté*, which on occasion heightens the sarcasm. Lien Chi accompanies the Man in Black to a
theatre to see an English play. Here is part of the
performance :—" I was going to second his remarks,
when my attention was engrossed by a new object; a
man came in balancing a straw upon his nose, and the
audience were clapping their hands in all the raptures of
applause. 'To what purpose,' cried I, 'does this unmeaning figure make his appearance? is he a part of
the plot?'—'Unmeaning do you call him?' replied my
friend in black; 'this is one of the most important
characters of the whole play; nothing pleases the
people more than seeing a straw balanced : there is a
great deal of meaning in a straw : there is something
suited to every apprehension in the sight ; and a fellow
possessed of talents like these is sure of making his
fortune.' The third act now began with an actor who
came to inform us that he was the villain of the play,
and intended to show strange things before all was
over. He was joined by another who seemed as much

disposed for mischief as he; their intrigues continued through this whole division. 'If that be a villain,' said I, 'he must be a very stupid one to tell his secrets without being asked; such soliloquies of late are never admitted in China.' The noise of clapping interrupted me once more; a child six years old was learning to dance on the stage, which gave the ladies and mandarins infinite satisfaction. 'I am sorry,' said I, 'to see the pretty creature so early learning so bad a trade; dancing being, I presume, as contemptible here as in China.'— 'Quite the reverse,' interrupted my companion; 'dancing is a very reputable and genteel employment here; men have a greater chance for encouragement from the merit of their heels than their heads. One who jumps up and flourishes his toes three times before he comes to the ground may have three hundred a year: he who flourishes them four times, gets four hundred; but he who arrives at five is inestimable, and may demand what salary he thinks proper. The female dancers, too, are valued for this sort of jumping and crossing; and it is a cant word amongst them, that she deserves most who shows highest. But the fourth act is begun; let us be attentive.' ''

The Man in Black here mentioned is one of the notable features of this series of papers. The mysterious person whose acquaintance the Chinaman made in Westminster Abbey, and who concealed such a wonderful goodness of heart under a rough and forbidding exterior, is a charming character indeed; and it is impossible to praise too highly the vein of subtle sarcasm in which he preaches worldly wisdom. But to assume that any part of his history which he disclosed

to the Chinaman was a piece of autobiographical
writing on the part of Goldsmith, is a very hazardous
thing. A writer of fiction must necessarily use such
materials as have come within his own experience; and
Goldsmith's experience—or his use of those materials—
was extremely limited: witness how often a pet fancy,
like his remembrance of *Johnny Armstrong's Last Good
Night*, is repeated. "That of these simple elements,"
writes Professor Masson, in his *Memoir of Goldsmith*,
prefixed to an edition of his works, "he made so many
charming combinations, really differing from each other,
and all, though suggested by fact, yet hung so sweetly
in an ideal air, proved what an artist he was, and was
better than much that is commonly called invention.
In short, if there is a sameness of effect in Goldsmith's
writings, it is because they consist of poetry and truth,
humour and pathos, from his own life, and the supply
from such a life as his was not inexhaustible."

The question of invention is easily disposed of. Any
child can invent a world transcending human experience
by the simple combination of ideas which are in themselves incongruous—a world in which the horses have
each five feet, in which the grass is blue and the sky
green, in which seas are balanced on the peaks of
mountains. The result is unbelievable and worthless.
But the writer of imaginative literature uses his own
experiences and the experiences of others, so that his
combination of ideas in themselves compatible shall
appear so natural and believable that the reader—
although these incidents and characters never did
actually exist—is as much interested in them as if they
had existed. The mischief of it is that the reader

sometimes thinks himself very clever, and, recognising a little bit of the story as having happened to the author, jumps to the conclusion that such and such a passage is necessarily autobiographical. Hence it is that Goldsmith has been hastily identified with the Philosophic Vagabond in the *Vicar of Wakefield,* and with the Man in Black in the *Citizen of the World.* That he may have used certain experiences in the one, and that he may perhaps have given in the other a sort of fancy sketch of a person suggested by some trait in his own character, is possible enough ; but further assertion of likeness is impossible. That the Man in Black had one of Goldsmith's little weaknesses is obvious enough : we find him just a trifle too conscious of his own kindliness and generosity. The Vicar of Wakefield himself is not without a spice of this amiable vanity. As for Goldsmith, every one must remember his reply to Griffiths' accusation : "No, sir, had I been a sharper, *had I been possessed of less good nature and native generosity,* I might surely now have been in better circumstances."

The Man in Black, in any case, is a delightful character. We detect the warm and generous nature even in his pretence of having acquired worldly wisdom : " I now therefore pursued a course of uninterrupted frugality, seldom wanted a dinner, and was consequently invited to twenty. I soon began to get the character of a saving hunks that had money, and insensibly grew into esteem. Neighbours have asked my advice in the disposal of their daughters ; and I have always taken care not to give any. I have contracted a friendship with an alderman, only by observing, that if we take a farthing

from a thousand pounds it will be a thousand pounds
no longer. I have been invited to a pawnbroker's
table, by pretending to hate gravy; and am now
actually upon treaty of marriage with a rich widow,
for only having observed that the bread was rising.
If ever I am asked a question, whether I know
it or not, instead of answering, I only smile and look
wise. If a charity is proposed I go about with the
hat, but put nothing in myself. If a wretch solicits my
pity, I observe that the world is filled with impostors,
and take a certain method of not being deceived by
never relieving. In short, I now find the truest way
of finding esteem, even from the indigent, is to give
away nothing, and thus have much in our power to
give." This is a very clever piece of writing, whether
it is in strict accordance with the character of the Man
in Black, or not. But there is in these *Public Ledger*
papers another sketch of character, which is not only
consistent in itself, and in every way admirable, but is
of still further interest to us when we remember that
at this time the various personages in the *Vicar of
Wakefield* were no doubt gradually assuming definite
form in Goldsmith's mind. It is in the figure of Mr.
Tibbs, introduced apparently at haphazard, but at once
taking possession of us by its quaint relief, that we
find Goldsmith showing a firmer hand in character-
drawing. With a few happy dramatic touches Mr.
Tibbs starts into life; he speaks for himself; he becomes one of the people whom we know. And yet,
with this concise and sharp portraiture of a human
being, look at the graceful, almost garrulous, ease of the
style :—

"Our pursuer soon came up and joined us with all the familiarity of an old acquaintance. 'My dear Drybone,' cries he, shaking my friend's hand, 'where have you been hiding this half a century? Positively I had fancied you were gone to cultivate matrimony and your estate in the country.' During the reply I had an opportunity of surveying the appearance of our new companion : his hat was pinched up with peculiar smartness ; his looks were pale, thin, and sharp ; round his neck he wore a broad black riband, and in his bosom a buckle studded with glass; his coat was trimmed with tarnished twist ; he wore by his side a sword with a black hilt ; and his stockings of silk, though newly washed, were grown yellow by long service. I was so much engaged with the peculiarity of his dress, that I attended only to the latter part of my friend's reply, in which he complimented Mr. Tibbs on the taste of his clothes and the bloom in his countenance. 'Pshaw, pshaw, Will,' cried the figure, 'no more of that, if you love me : you know I hate flattery, —on my soul I do ; and yet, to be sure, an intimacy with the great will improve one's appearance, and a course of venison will fatten ; and yet, faith, I despise the great as much as you do ; but there are a great many damn'd honest fellows among them, and we must not quarrel with one half, because the other wants weeding. If they were all such as my Lord Mudler, one of the most good-natured creatures that ever squeezed a lemon, I should myself be among the number of their admirers. I was yesterday to dine at the Duchess of Piccadilly's. My lord was there. "Ned," says he to me, "Ned," says he, "I'll hold gold to silver,

I can tell you where you were poaching last night."
"Poaching, my lord?" says I: "faith, you have
missed already; for I staid at home and let the girls
poach for me. That's my way: I take a fine woman
as some animals do their prey—stand still, and, swoop,
they fall into my mouth."' 'Ah, Tibbs, thou art a
happy fellow,' cried my companion, with looks of
infinite pity; 'I hope your fortune is as much improved as your understanding, in such company?'
'Improved!' replied the other: 'you shall know,—
but let it go no farther—a great secret—five hundred
a year to begin with—my lord's word of honour for it.
His lordship took me down in his own chariot yesterday,
and we had a *tête-à-tête* dinner in the country, where
we talked of nothing else.'—'I fancy you forget, sir,'
cried I; 'you told us but this moment of your dining
yesterday in town.'—'Did I say so?' replied he,
coolly; 'to be sure, if I said so, it was so. Dined in
town! egad, now I do remember, I did dine in town;
but I dined in the country too; for you must know,
my boys, I ate two dinners. By the bye, I am grown
as nice as the devil in my eating. I'll tell you a
pleasant affair about that: we were a select party of
us to dine at Lady Grogram's,—an affected piece, but
let it go no farther—a secret.—Well, there happened
to be no asafœtida in the sauce to a turkey, upon which,
says I, I'll hold a thousand guineas, and say done, first,
that—But, dear Drybone, you are an honest creature;
lend me half-a-crown for a minute or two, or so, just
till ——; but hearkee, ask me for it the next time
we meet, or it may be twenty to one but I forget to
pay you.'"

Returning from these performances to the author of them, we find him a busy man of letters, becoming more and more in request among the booksellers, and obtaining recognition among his fellow-writers.   He had moved into better lodgings in Wine Office Court (1760-2) ; and it was here that he entertained at supper, as has already been mentioned, no less distinguished guests than Bishop, then Mr., Percy, and Dr., then Mr., Johnson. Every one has heard of the surprise of Percy, on calling for Johnson, to find the great Cham dressed with quite unusual smartness.   On asking the cause of this " singular transformation," Johnson replied, " Why, sir, I hear that Goldsmith, who is a very great sloven, justifies his disregard of cleanliness and decency by quoting my practice ; and I am desirous this night to show him a better example."   That Goldsmith profited by this example—though the tailors did not—is clear enough.   At times, indeed, he blossomed out into the splendours of a dandy ; and laughed at himself for doing so.   But whether he was in gorgeous or in mean attire, he remained the same sort of happy-go-lucky creature ; working hard by fits and starts ; continually getting money in advance from the booksellers ; enjoying the present hour ; and apparently happy enough when not pressed by debt.   That he should have been thus pressed was no necessity of the case ; at all events we need not on this score begin now to abuse the book-sellers or the public of that day.   We may dismiss once for all the oft-repeated charges of ingratitude and neglect.

When Goldsmith was writing those letters in the *Public Ledger*—with " pleasure and instruction for others," Mr. Forster says, " though at the cost of suffering to

himself "—he was receiving for them alone what would
be equivalent in our day to £200 a year.   No man can
affirm that £200 a year is not amply sufficient for all the
material wants of life.   Of course there are fine things in
the world that that amount of annual wage cannot purchase.   It is a fine thing to sit on the deck of a yacht on
a summer's day, and watch the far islands shining over the
blue ; it is a fine thing to drive four-in-hand to Ascot—
if you can do it ; it is a fine thing to cower breathless
behind a rock and find a splendid stag coming slowly
within sure range.   But these things are not necessary
to human happiness : it is possible to do without them
and yet not "suffer."   Even if Goldsmith had given
half of his substance away to the poor, there was enough
left to cover all the necessary wants of a human being ;
and if he chose so to order his affairs as to incur the
suffering of debt, why, that was his own business,
about which nothing further needs be said.   It is to be
suspected, indeed, that he did not care to practise those
excellent maxims of prudence and frugality which he
frequently preached ; but the world is not much concerned about that now.   If Goldsmith had received ten
times as much money as the booksellers gave him, he
would still have died in debt.   And it is just possible
that we may exaggerate Goldsmith's sensitiveness on
this score.   He had had a life-long familiarity with
duns and borrowing ; and seemed very contented when
the exigency of the hour was tided over.   An angry
landlady is unpleasant, and an arrest is awkward ; but
in comes an opportune guinea, and the bottle of Madeira
is opened forthwith.

In these rooms in Wine Office Court, and at the

suggestion or entreaty of Newbery, Goldsmith produced
a good deal of miscellaneous writing—pamphlets, tracts,
compilations, and what not—of a more or less market-
able kind. It can only be surmised that by this time
he may have formed some idea of producing a book not
solely meant for the market, and that the characters in
the *Vicar of Wakefield* were already engaging his attention ; but the surmise becomes probable enough when
we remember that his project of writing the *Traveller*,
which was not published till 1764, had been formed as
far back as 1755, while he was wandering aimlessly
about Europe, and that a sketch of the poem was actually
forwarded by him then to his brother Henry in Ireland.
But in the meantime this hack-work, and the habits of
life connected with it, began to tell on Goldsmith's
health ; and so, for a time, he left London (1762), and
went to Tunbridge and then to Bath. It is scarcely
possible that his modest fame had preceded him to the
latter place of fashion ; but it may be that the distinguished folk of the town received this friend of the great
Dr. Johnson with some small measure of distinction ;
for we find that his next published work, *The Life of
Richard Nash, Esq.*, is respectfully dedicated to the
Right Worshipful the Mayor, Recorder, Aldermen, and
Common Council of the City of Bath. The Life of the
recently deceased Master of Ceremonies was published
anonymously (1762) ; but it was generally understood to
be Goldsmith's ; and indeed the secret of the authorship is revealed in every successive line. Among the
minor writings of Goldsmith there is none more delightful than this : the mock-heroic gravity, the half-familiar
contemptuous good-nature with which he composes

this Funeral March of a Marionette, are extremely
whimsical and amusing. And then what an admirable
picture we get of fashionable English society in the
beginning of the eighteenth century, when Bath and
Nash were alike in the heyday of their glory—the fine
ladies with their snuff-boxes, and their passion for play,
and their extremely effective language when they got
angry ; young bucks come to flourish away their money,
and gain by their losses the sympathy of the fair ;
sharpers on the look-out for guineas, and adventurers
on the look-out for weak-minded heiresses ; duchesses
writing letters in the most doubtful English, and chair-
men swearing at any one who dared to walk home on
foot at night.

No doubt the Life of Beau Nash was a bookseller's
book ; and it was made as attractive as possible by the
recapitulation of all sorts of romantic stories about
Miss S——n, and Mr. C——e, and Captain K——g ;
but throughout we find the historian very much inclined to laugh at his hero, and only refraining now and
again in order to record in serious language traits
indicative of the real goodness of disposition of that fop
and gambler. And the fine ladies and gentlemen, who
lived in that atmosphere of scandal, and intrigue, and
gambling, are also from time to time treated to a little
decorous and respectful raillery. Who does not remember the famous laws of polite breeding written out
by Mr. Nash—Goldsmith hints that neither Mr. Nash
nor his fair correspondent at Blenheim, the Duchess of
Marlborough, excelled in English composition—for the
guidance of the ladies and gentlemen who were under
the sway of the King of Bath ?   "But were we to give

laws to a nursery, we should make them childish laws,"
Goldsmith writes gravely. " His statutes, though stupid,
were addressed to fine gentlemen and ladies, and were
probably received with sympathetic approbation. It is
certain they were in general religiously observed by his
subjects, and executed by him with impartiality ; neither
rank nor fortune shielded the refractory from his resentment." Nash, however, was not content with prose
in enforcing good manners. Having waged deadly war
against the custom of wearing boots, and having found
his ordinary armoury of no avail against the obduracy
of the country squires, he assailed them in the im-
passioned language of poetry, and produced the following
"Invitation to the Assembly," which, as Goldsmith
remarks, was highly relished by the nobility at Bath on
account of its keenness, severity, and particularly its
good rhymes.

> " Come, one and all, to Hoyden Hall,
> For there's the assembly this night ;
>   None but prude fools
>   Mind manners and rules ;
> We Hoydens do decency slight.
>   Come, trollops and slatterns,
>   Cocked hats and white aprons,
> This best our modesty suits ;
>   For why should not we
>   In dress be as free
> As Hogs-Norton squires in boots ? "

The sarcasm was too much for the squires, who yielded
in a body ; and when any stranger through inadvertence
presented himself in the assembly-rooms in boots, Nash
was so completely master of the situation that he would

politely step up to the intruder and suggest that he had forgotten his horse.

Goldsmith does not magnify the intellectual capacity of his hero; but he gives him credit for a sort of rude wit that was sometimes effective enough. His physician, for example, having called on him to see whether he had followed a prescription that had been sent him the previous day, was greeted in this fashion: "Followed your prescription? No. Egad, if I had, I should have broken my neck, for I flung it out of the two pair of stairs window." For the rest, this diverting biography contains some excellent warnings against the vice of gambling; with a particular account of the manner in which the Government of the day tried by statute after statute to suppress the tables at Tunbridge and Bath, thereby only driving the sharpers to new subterfuges. That the Beau was in alliance with sharpers, or, at least, that he was a sleeping partner in the firm, his biographer admits; but it is urged on his behalf that he was the most generous of winners, and again and again interfered to prevent the ruin of some gambler by whose folly he would himself have profited. His constant charity was well known; the money so lightly come by was at the disposal of any one who could prefer a piteous tale. Moreover he made no scruple about exacting from others that charity which they could well afford. One may easily guess who was the duchess mentioned in the following story of Goldsmith's narration:—

"The sums he gave and collected for the Hospital were great, and his manner of doing it was no less admirable. I am told that he was once collecting money in Wiltshire's room for that purpose, when a lady entered, who is more remarkable for her wit than her charity, and not being able to pass by him unobserved, she gave him a pat with her fan, and said, 'You must put down a trifle for me, Nash, for I have no money in my pocket.' 'Yes, madam,' says he, 'that I will with pleasure, if your grace will tell me when to stop;' then taking an handful of guineas out of his pocket, he began to tell them into his white hat — 'One, two, three, four, five——' 'Hold, hold!' says the duchess, 'consider what you are about.' 'Consider your rank and fortune, madam,' says Nash, and continues telling —'six, seven, eight, nine, ten.' Here the duchess called again, and seemed angry. 'Pray compose yourself, madam,' cried Nash, 'and don't interrupt the work of charity,—eleven, twelve, thirteen, fourteen, fifteen.' Here the duchess stormed, and caught hold of his hand. 'Peace, madam,' says Nash, 'you shall have your name written in letters of gold, madam, and upon the front of the building, madam,—sixteen, seventeen, eighteen, nineteen, twenty.' 'I won't pay a farthing more,' says the duchess. 'Charity hides a multitude of sins,' replies Nash,— 'twenty-one, twenty-two, twenty-three, twenty-four, twenty-five.' 'Nash,' says she, 'I protest you frighten me out of my wits. L—d, I shall die!' 'Madam, you will never die with doing good; and if you do, it will be the better for you,' answered Nash, and was about to proceed; but perceiving her grace had lost all patience, a parley ensued, when he, after much altercation, agreed to stop his hand and compound with her grace for thirty guineas. The duchess, however, seemed displeased the whole evening, and when he came to the

F

table where she was playing, bid him, 'Stand farther,
an ugly devil, for she hated the sight of him.'   But her
grace afterwards having a run of good luck, called Nash
to her.   'Come,' says she, 'I will be friends with you,
though you are a fool; and to let you see I am not
angry, there is ten guineas more for your charity.   But
this I insist on, that neither my name nor the sum shall
be mentioned.' "

At the ripe age of eighty-seven the "beau of three
generations " breathed his last (1761) ; and, though he
had fallen into poor ways, there were those alive who
remembered his former greatness, and who chronicled
it in a series of epitaphs and poetical lamentations.
" One thing is common almost with all of them," says
Goldsmith, "and that is that Venus, Cupid, and the
Graces are commanded to weep, and that Bath shall
never find such another."   These effusions are forgotten
now; and so would Beau Nash be also, but for this
biography, which, no doubt meant merely for the book-
market of the day, lives and is of permanent value by
reason of the charm of its style, its pervading humour,
and the vivacity of its descriptions of the fashionable
follies of the eighteenth century.   *Nullum fere genus
scribendi non tetigit.   Nullum quod tetigit non ornavit.*
Who but Goldsmith could have written so delightful
a book about such a poor creature as Beau Nash?

CHAPTER VIII.

It was no doubt owing to Newbery that Goldsmith, after his return to London, was induced to abandon, temporarily or altogether, his apartments in Wine Office Court, and take lodgings in the house of a Mrs. Fleming, who lived somewhere or other in Islington. Newbery had rooms in Canonbury House, a curious old building that still exists; and it may have occurred to the publisher that Goldsmith, in this suburban district, would not only be nearer him for consultation and so forth, but also might pay more attention to his duties than when he was among the temptations of Fleet Street. Goldsmith was working industriously in the service of Newbery at this time (1763-4) ; in fact, so completely was the bookseller in possession of the hack, that Goldsmith's board and lodging in Mrs. Fleming's house, arranged for at £50 a year, was paid by Newbery himself. Writing prefaces, revising new editions, contributing reviews— this was the sort of work he undertook, with more or less content, as the equivalent of the modest sums Mr. Newbery disbursed for him or handed over as pocket-money. In the midst of all this drudgery he was now secretly engaged on work that aimed at something

F 2

higher than mere payment of bed and board. The
smooth lines of the *Traveller* were receiving further
polish; the gentle-natured *Vicar* was writing his simple,
quaint, tender story. And no doubt Goldsmith was
spurred to try something better than hack-work by the
associations that he was now forming, chiefly under the
wise and benevolent friendship of Johnson.

Anxious always to be thought well of, he was now beginning to meet people whose approval was worthy of being
sought. He had been introduced to Reynolds. He had
become the friend of Hogarth. He had even made the
acquaintance of Mr. Boswell, from Scotland. Moreover,
he had been invited to become one of the original members
of the famous Club of which so much has been written;
his fellow-members being Reynolds, Johnson, Burke,
Hawkins, Beauclerk, Bennet Langton, and Dr. Nugent.
It is almost certain that it was at Johnson's instigation that he had been admitted into this choice fellow-
ship. Long before either the *Traveller* or the *Vicar* had
been heard of, Johnson had perceived the literary genius
that obscurely burned in the uncouth figure of this
Irishman; and was anxious to impress on others Goldsmith's claims to respect and consideration. In the
minute record kept by Boswell of his first evening with
Johnson at the Mitre Tavern, we find Johnson saying,
" Dr. Goldsmith is one of the first men we now have as
an author, and he is a very worthy man too. He has
been loose in his principles, but he is coming right."
Johnson took walks with Goldsmith; did him the honour
of disputing with him on all occasions; bought a copy of
the *Life of Nash* when it appeared—an unusual compliment for one author to pay another, in their day or in

ours ; allowed him to call on Miss Williams, the blind old
lady in Bolt Court ; and generally was his friend, coun-
sellor, and champion.   Accordingly, when Mr. Boswell
entertained the great Cham to supper at the Mitre—a
sudden quarrel with his landlord having made it impossible for him to order the banquet at his own house—
he was careful to have Dr. Goldsmith of the company.
His guests that evening were Johnson, Goldsmith, Davies
(the actor and bookseller who had conferred on Boswell
the invaluable favour of an introduction to Johnson),
Mr. Eccles, and the Rev. Mr. Ogilvie, a Scotch poet
who deserves our gratitude because it was his inoppor-
tune patriotism that provoked, on this very evening,
the memorable epigram about the high-road leading to
England.   "Goldsmith," says Boswell, who had not
got over his envy at Goldsmith's being allowed to visit
the blind old pensioner in Bolt-court, "as usual, en-
deavoured with too much eagerness to *shine*, and disputed
very warmly with Johnson against the well-known
maxim of the British constitution, ' The king can do no
wrong.' "   It was a dispute not so much about facts as
about phraseology ; and, indeed, there seems to be no
great warmth in the expressions used on either side.
Goldsmith affirmed that " what was morally false could
not be politically true ; " and that, in short, the king
could by the misuse of his regal power do wrong.
Johnson replied, that, in such a case, the immediate
agents of the king were the persons to be tried and
punished for the offence.   "The king, though he should
command, cannot force a judge to condemn a man
unjustly ; therefore it is the judge whom we prosecute
and punish."   But when he stated that the king "is

above everything, and there is no power by which he can
be tried," he was surely forgetting an important chapter
in English history. "What did Cromwell do for his
country?" he himself asked, during his subsequent visit
to Scotland, of old Auchinleck, Boswell's father. "God,
Doctor," replied the vile Whig, "*he garred kings ken
they had a lith in their necks.*"

For some time after this evening Goldsmith drops
out of Boswell's famous memoir; perhaps the compiler
was not anxious to give him too much prominence.
They had not liked each other from the outset.
Boswell, vexed by the greater intimacy of Goldsmith
with Johnson, called him a blunderer, a feather-brained
person; and described his appearance in no flattering
terms. Goldsmith, on the other hand, on being asked
who was this Scotch cur that followed Johnson's heels,
answered, "He is not a cur : you are too severe—he is
only a bur. Tom Davies flung him at Johnson in sport,
and he has the faculty of sticking." Boswell would
probably have been more tolerant of Goldsmith as a
rival, if he could have known that on a future day he
was to have Johnson all to himself—to carry him to
remote wilds and exhibit him as a portentous literary
phenomenon to Highland lairds. It is true that
Johnson, at an early period of his acquaintance with
Boswell, did talk vaguely about a trip to the Hebrides;
but the young Scotch idolater thought it was all too
good to be true. The mention of Sir James Macdonald,
says Boswell, "led us to talk of the Western Islands
of Scotland, to visit which he expressed a wish that
then appeared to me a very romantic fancy, which I
little thought would be afterwards realised. He told

me that his father had put Martin's account of those
islands into his hands when he was very young, and
that he was highly pleased with it; that he was particularly struck with the St. Kilda man's notion that
the high church of Glasgow had been hollowed out of
a rock; a circumstance to which old Mr. Johnson had
directed his attention." Unfortunately Goldsmith not
only disappears from the pages of Boswell's biography
at this time, but also in great measure from the ken
of his companions. He was deeply in debt; no doubt
the fine clothes he had been ordering from Mr. Filby
in order that he might "shine" among those notable
persons, had something to do with it; he had tried the
patience of the booksellers; and he had been devoting
a good deal of time to work not intended to elicit
immediate payment. The most patient endeavours to
trace out his changes of lodgings, and the fugitive
writings that kept him in daily bread, have not been
very successful. It is to be presumed that Goldsmith
had occasionally to go into hiding to escape from his
creditors; and so was missed from his familiar haunts.
We only reach daylight again, to find Goldsmith being
under threat of arrest from his landlady; and for the
particulars of this famous affair it is necessary to return
to Boswell.

Boswell was not in London at that time; but his
account was taken down subsequently from Johnson's
narration; and his accuracy in other matters, his extraordinary memory, and scrupulous care, leave no doubt
in the mind that his version of the story is to be preferred to those of Mrs. Piozzi and Sir John Hawkins.
We may take it that these are Johnson's own words:—

"I received one morning a message from poor Goldsmith that he was in great distress, and, as it was not in his power to come to me, begging that I would come to him as soon as possible. I sent him a guinea, and promised to come to him directly. I accordingly went as soon as I was dressed, and found that his landlady had arrested him for his rent, at which he was in a violent passion. I perceived that he had already changed my guinea, and had got a bottle of Madeira and a glass before him. I put the cork into the bottle, desired he would be calm, and began to talk to him of the means by which he might be extricated. He then told me that he had a novel ready for the press, which he produced to me. I looked into it, and saw its mérit; told the landlady I should soon return; and, having gone to a bookseller, sold it for £60. I brought Goldsmith the money, and he discharged his rent, not without rating his landlady in a high tone for having used him so ill."

We do not know who this landlady was—it cannot now be made out whether the incident occurred at Islington, or in the rooms that Goldsmith partially occupied in the Temple; but even if Mrs. Fleming be the landlady in question, she was deserving neither of Goldsmith's rating nor of the reprimands that have been bestowed upon her by later writers. Mrs. Fleming had been exceedingly kind to Goldsmith. Again and again in her bills we find items significantly marked £0 0s. 0d. And if her accounts with her lodger did get hopelessly into arrear; and if she was annoyed by seeing him go out in fine clothes to sup at the Mitre; and if, at length, her patience gave way, and she determined to have her rights in one way or another, she was no worse

than landladies—who are only human beings, and not
divinely appointed protectresses of genius—ordinarily
are. Mrs. Piozzi says that when Johnson came back
with the money, Goldsmith "called the woman of the
house directly to partake of punch, and pass their time
in merriment." This would be a dramatic touch; but,
after Johnson's quietly corking the bottle of Madeira,
it is more likely that no such thing occurred; especially
as Boswell quotes the statement as an "extreme in-
accuracy."

The novel which Johnson had taken away and sold
to Francis Newbery, a nephew of the elder bookseller,
was, as every one knows, the *Vicar of Wakefield*. That
Goldsmith, amidst all his pecuniary distresses, should
have retained this piece in his desk, instead of pawning
or promising it to one of his bookselling patrons, points
to but one conclusion—that he was building high hopes
on it, and was determined to make it as good as lay
within his power. Goldsmith put an anxious finish into
all his better work; perhaps that is the secret of the
graceful ease that is now apparent in every line. Any
young writer who may imagine that the power of clear
and concise literary expression comes by nature, cannot
do better than study, in Mr. Cunningham's big collection of Goldsmith's writings, the continual and minute
alterations which the author considered necessary even
after the first edition—sometimes when the second and
third editions—had been published. Many of these,
especially in the poetical works, were merely improve-
ments in sound as suggested by a singularly sensitive
ear, as when he altered the line

　　　"Amidst the ruin, heedless of the dead,"

which had appeared in the first three editions of the *Traveller*, into

"There in the ruin, heedless of the dead,"

which appeared in the fourth. But the majority of the omissions and corrections were prompted by a careful taste, that abhorred everything redundant or slovenly. It has been suggested that when Johnson carried off the *Vicar of Wakefield* to Francis Newbery, the manuscript was not quite finished, but had to be completed afterwards. There was at least plenty of time for that. Newbery does not appear to have imagined that he had obtained a prize in the lottery of literature. He paid the £60 for it—clearly on the assurance of the great father of learning of the day, that there was merit in the little story—somewhere about the end of 1764; but the tale was not issued to the public until March, 1766. "And, sir," remarked Johnson to Boswell, with regard to the sixty pounds, "a sufficient price too, when it was sold; for then the fame of Goldsmith had not been elevated, as it afterwards was, by his *Traveller*; and the bookseller had such faint hopes of profit by his bargain, that he kept the manuscript by him a long time, and did not publish it till after the *Traveller* had appeared. Then, to be sure, it was accidentally worth more money."

CHAPTER IX.

THIS poem of the *Traveller*, the fruit of much secret
labour and the consummation of the hopes of many
years, was lying completed in Goldsmith's desk when
the incident of the arrest occurred; and the elder
Newbery had undertaken to publish it. Then, as at
other times, Johnson lent this wayward child of genius
a friendly hand. He read over the proof-sheets for
Goldsmith; was so kind as to put in a line here or
there where he thought fit; and prepared a notice of the
poem for the *Critical Review*. The time for the appearance of this new claimant for poetical honours was
propitious. "There was perhaps no point in the
century," says Professor Masson, "when the British
Muse, such as she had come to be, was doing less, or
had so nearly ceased to do anything, or to have any
good opinion of herself, as precisely about the year
1764. Young was dying; Gray was recluse and in-
dolent; Johnson had long given over his metrical
experimentations on any except the most inconsiderable
scale; Akenside, Armstrong, Smollett, and others less
known, had pretty well revealed the amount of their

worth in poetry; and Churchill, after his ferocious blaze
of what was really rage and declamation in metre,
though conventionally it was called poetry, was prematurely defunct.   Into this lull came Goldsmith's
short but carefully finished poem."   "There has not
been so fine a poem since Pope's time," remarked
Johnson to Boswell, on the very first evening after the
return of young Auchinleck to London.   It would have
been no matter for surprise had Goldsmith dedicated this
first work that he published under his own name to
Johnson, who had for so long been his constant friend
and adviser; and such a dedication would have carried
weight in certain quarters.   But there was a finer touch
in Goldsmith's thought of inscribing the book to his
brother Henry; and no doubt the public were surprised
and pleased to find a poor devil of an author dedicating
a work to an Irish parson with £40 a year, from whom
he could not well expect any return.   It will be
remembered that it was to this brother Henry that
Goldsmith, ten years before, had sent the first sketch
of the poem; and now the wanderer,

> " Remote, unfriended, melancholy, slow."

declares how his heart untravelled

> " Still to my brother turns, with ceaseless pain,
>   And drags at each remove a lengthening chain."

The very first line of the poem strikes a key-note—
there is in it a pathetic thrill of distance, and regret, and
longing; and it has the soft musical sound that pervades
the whole composition.   It is exceedingly interesting to

note, as has already been mentioned, how Goldsmith
altered and altered these lines until he had got them
full of gentle vowel sounds. Where, indeed, in the
English language could one find more graceful melody
than this?—

> " The naked negro, panting at the line,
> Boasts of his golden sands and palmy wine,
> Basks in the glare, or stems the tepid wave,
> And thanks his gods for all the good they gave."

It has been observed also that Goldsmith was the first
to introduce into English poetry sonorous American
— or rather Indian—names, as when he writes in this
poem,

> " Where wild Oswego spreads her swamps around,
> And Niagara stuns with thundering sound,"

—and if it be charged against him that he ought to
have known the proper accentuation of Niagara, it may
be mentioned as a set-off that Sir Walter Scott, in
dealing with his own country, mis-accentuated " Glena-
ládale," to say nothing of his having made of Roseneath
an island. Another characteristic of the *Traveller* is
the extraordinary choiceness and conciseness of the
diction, which, instead of suggesting pedantry or affec-
tation, betrays on the contrary nothing but a delightful
ease and grace.

The English people are very fond of good English;
and thus it is that couplets from the *Traveller* and the
Deserted Village have come into the common stock of
our language, and that sometimes not so much on
account of the ideas they convey, as through their

singular precision of epithet and musical sound. It is
enough to make the angels weep, to find such a couplet
as this—

> " Cheerful at morn, he wakes from short repose,
>   Breasts the keen air, and carols as he goes,"

murdered in several editions of Goldsmith's works by
the substitution of the commonplace " breathes " for
" breasts "—and that, after Johnson had drawn particular
attention to the line by quoting it in his Dictionary.
Perhaps, indeed, it may be admitted that the literary
charm of the *Traveller* is more apparent than the value
of any doctrine, however profound or ingenious, which
the poem was supposed to inculcate. We forget all about
the " particular principle of happiness " possessed by
each European state, in listening to the melody of the
singer, and in watching the successive and delightful
pictures that he calls up before the imagination.

> " As in those domes where Cæsars once bore sway,
>   Defaced by time, and tottering in decay,
>   There in the ruin, heedless of the dead,
>   The shelter-seeking peasant builds his shed ;
>   And, wondering man could want the larger pile,
>   Exults, and owns his cottage with a smile."

Then notice the blaze of patriotic idealism that bursts
forth when he comes to talk of England. What sort of
England had he been familiar with when he was con-
sorting with the meanest wretches—the poverty stricken,
the sick, and squalid—in those Fleet-Street dens ? But
it is an England of bright streams and spacious lawns

of which he writes; and as for the people who inhabit
the favoured land—

> " Stern o'er each bosom reason holds her state,
>   With daring aims irregularly great;
>   Pride in their port, defiance in their eye,
>   I see the lords of human kind pass by."

" Whenever I write anything," Goldsmith had said,
with a humorous exaggeration which Boswell, as usual,
takes *au sérieux*, " the public *make a point* to know
nothing about it." But we have Johnson's testimony
to the fact that the *Traveller* " brought him into high
reputation." No wonder. When the great Cham declares it to be the finest poem published since the time
of Pope, we are irresistibly forced to think of the
Essay on Man. What a contrast there is between that
tedious and stilted effort, and this clear burst of bird-
song! The *Traveller*, however, did not immediately
become popular. It was largely talked about, naturally,
among Goldsmith's friends; and Johnson would scarcely
suffer any criticism of it. At a dinner given long afterwards at Sir Joshua Reynolds's, and fully reported by the
invaluable Boswell, Reynolds remarked, "I was glad
to hear Charles Fox say it was one of the finest poems
in the English language." "Why were you glad?"
said Langton. "You surely had no doubt of this
before?" Hereupon Johnson struck in: "No; the
merit of the *Traveller* is so well established, that
Mr. Fox's praise cannot augment it, nor his censure
diminish it." And he went on to say—Goldsmith
having died and got beyond the reach of all critics and
creditors some three or four years before this time—

" Goldsmith was a man who, whatever he wrote, did it better than any other man could do. He deserved a place in Westminster Abbey; and every year he lived would have deserved it better."

Presently people began to talk about the new poem. A second edition was issued; a third; a fourth. It is not probable that Goldsmith gained any pecuniary benefit from the growing popularity of the little book; but he had " struck for honest fame," and that was now coming to him. He even made some slight acquaintance with "the great ; " and here occurs an incident which is one of many that account for the love that the English people have for Goldsmith. It appears that Hawkins, calling one day on the Earl of Northumberland, found the author of the *Traveller* waiting in the outer room, in response to an invitation. Hawkins, having finished his own business, retired, but lingered about until the interview between Goldsmith and his lordship was over, having some curiosity about the result. Here follows Goldsmith's report to Hawkins. " His lordship told me he had read my poem, and was much delighted with it ; that he was going to be Lord-lieutenant of Ireland ; and that, hearing that I was a native of that country, he should be glad to do me any kindness." "What did you answer ? " says Hawkins, no doubt expecting to hear of some application for pension or post. " Why," said Goldsmith, " I could say nothing but that I had a brother there, a clergyman, that stood in need of help," —and then he explained to Hawkins that he looked to the booksellers for support, and was not inclined to place dependence on the promises of great men. " Thus did this idiot in the affairs of the world," adds Hawkins, with a fatuity that is quite remarkable in its way, "trifle with his fortunes, and put back the hand that was held out to assist him ! Other offers of a like kind he either rejected or failed to improve, contenting himself with the patronage of one nobleman, whose mansion afforded him the delights of a splendid table and a retreat for a few days from the metropolis." It is a great pity we have not a description from the same pen of Johnson's insolent ingratitude in flinging the pair of boots down stairs.

CHAPTER X.

MISCELLANEOUS WRITING.

BUT one pecuniary result of this growing fame was a joint offer on the part of Griffin and Newbery of £20 for a selection from his printed essays; and this selection was forthwith made and published, with a preface written for the occasion. Here at once we can see that Goldsmith takes firmer ground. There is an air of confidence—of gaiety, even—in his address to the public; although, as usual, accompanied by a whimsical mock-modesty that is extremely odd and effective. "Whatever right I have to complain of the public," he says, "they can, as yet, have no just reason to complain of me. If I have written dull Essays, they have hitherto treated them as dull Essays. Thus far we are at least upon par, and until they think fit to make me their humble debtor by praise, I am resolved not to lose a single inch of my self-importance. Instead, therefore, of attempting to establish a credit amongst them, it will perhaps be wiser to apply to some more distant correspondent; and as my drafts are in some danger of being protested at home, it may not be imprudent, upon this occasion, to draw my bills upon Posterity.

" MR. POSTERITY,

" SIR,—Nine hundred and ninety-nine years after sight
hereof pay the bearer, or order, a thousand pounds worth
of praise, free from all deductions whatsoever, it being
a commodity that will then be very serviceable to him,
and place it to the account of, &c."

The bill is not yet due ; but there can in the meantime
be no harm in discounting it so far as to say that these
Essays deserve very decided praise.   They deal with all
manner of topics, matters of fact, matters of imagination,
humorous descriptions, learned criticisms ; and then,
whenever the entertainer thinks he is becoming dull, he
suddenly tells a quaint little story and walks off amidst
the laughter he knows he has produced.   It is not a very
ambitious or sonorous sort of literature ; but it was
admirably fitted for its aim—the passing of the
immediate hour in an agreeable and fairly intellectual
way.   One can often see, no doubt, that these Essays
are occasionally written in a more or less perfunctory
fashion, the writer not being moved by much enthusiasm in his subject ; but even then a quaint literary
grace seldom fails to atone, as when, writing about the
English clergy, and complaining that they do not
sufficiently in their addresses stoop to mean capacities,
he says—" Whatever may become of the higher orders
of mankind, who are generally possessed of collateral
motives to virtue, the vulgar should be particularly
regarded, whose behaviour in civil life is totally hinged
upon their hopes and fears.   Those who constitute the
basis of the great fabric of society should be particularly
regarded ; for in policy, as in architecture, ruin is most
fatal when it begins from the bottom."   There was,

G 2

indeed, throughout Goldsmith's miscellaneous writing
much more common sense than might have been expected
from a writer who was supposed to have none.

As regards his chance criticisms on dramatic and
poetical literature, these are generally found to be incisive and just ; while sometimes they exhibit a wholesome
disregard of mere tradition and authority. " Milton's
translation of Horace's Ode to Pyrrha," he says, for
example, " is universally known and generally admired,
in our opinion much above its merit." If the present
writer might for a moment venture into such an arena,
he would express the honest belief that that translation
is the very worst translation that was ever made of
anything. But there is the happy rendering of *simplex
munditiis*, which counts for much.

By this time Goldsmith had also written his charming ballad of *Edwin and Angelina*, which was privately
"printed for the amusement of the Countess of Northumberland," and which afterwards appeared in the
Vicar of Wakefield. It seems clear enough that this
quaint and pathetic piece was suggested by an old ballad
beginning,

> " Gentle heardsman, tell to me,
> Of curtesy I thee pray,
> Unto the towne of Walsingham
> Which is the right and ready way,"

which Percy had shown to Goldsmith, and which, patched
up, subsequently appeared in the *Reliques*. But Goldsmith's ballad is original enough to put aside all the
discussion about plagiarism which was afterwards started.

In the old fragment the weeping pilgrim receives directions from the herdsman, and goes on her way, and we
hear of her no more; in *Edwin and Angelina* the
forlorn and despairing maiden suddenly finds herself
confronted by the long-lost lover whom she had so
cruelly used. This is the dramatic touch that reveals
the hand of the artist. And here again it is curious to
note the care with which Goldsmith repeatedly revised
his writings. The ballad originally ended with these
two stanzas : —

> " Here amidst sylvan bowers we'll rove,
>   From lawn to woodland stray ;
>   Blest as the songsters of the grove,
>   And innocent as they.

> " To all that want, and all that wail,
>   Our pity shall be given,
>   And when this life of love shall fail,
>   We'll love again in heaven."

But subsequently it must have occurred to the author
that, the dramatic disclosure once made, and the lovers
restored to each other, any lingering over the scene only
weakened the force of the climax ; hence these stanzas
were judiciously excised. It may be doubted, however,
whether the original version of the last couplet :

> " And the last sigh that rends the heart
>   Shall break thy Edwin's too,"

was improved by being altered into

> " The sigh that rends thy constant heart
>   Shall break thy Edwin's too."

Meanwhile Goldsmith had resorted to hack-work
again ; nothing being expected from the *Vicar of Wakefield*, now lying in Newbery's shop, for that had been
paid for, and his expenses were increasing, as became
his greater station.   In the interval between the
publication of the *Traveller* and of the *Vicar*, he moved
into better chambers in Garden Court ; he hired a man-
servant, he blossomed out into very fine clothes.   Indeed, so effective did his first suit seem to be—the
purple silk small-clothes, the scarlet roquelaure, the
wig, sword, and gold-headed cane—that, as Mr. Forster
says, he "amazed his friends with no less than three
similar suits, not less expensive, in the next six months."
Part of this display was no doubt owing to a suggestion
from Reynolds that Goldsmith, having a medical degree,
might just as well add the practice of a physician to
his literary work, to magnify his social position.   Goldsmith, always willing to please his friends, acceded ;
but his practice does not appear to have been either
extensive or long-continued.   It is said that he drew
out a prescription for a certain Mrs. Sidebotham which
so appalled the apothecary that he refused to make it
up ; and that, as the lady sided with the apothecary, he
threw up the case and his profession at the same time. If
it was money Goldsmith wanted, he was not likely to get
it in that way ; he had neither the appearance nor the
manner fitted to humour the sick and transform healthy
people into valetudinarians. If it was the esteem of his
friends and popularity outside that circle, he was soon
to acquire enough of both.   On the 27th March, 1766,
fifteen months after the appearance of the *Traveller*,
the *Vicar of Wakefield* was published.

CHAPTER XI.

THE *Vicar of Wakefield*, considered structurally, follows the lines of the Book of Job. You take a good man, overwhelm him with successive misfortunes, show the pure flame of his soul burning in the midst of the darkness, and then, as the reward of his patience and fortitude and submission, restore him gradually to happiness, with even larger flocks and herds than before. The machinery by which all this is brought about is, in the *Vicar of Wakefield*, the weak part of the story. The plot is full of wild improbabilities; in fact, the expedients by which all the members of the family are brought together and made happy at the same time, are nothing short of desperate. It is quite clear, too, that the author does not know what to make of the episode of Olivia and her husband; they are allowed to drop through; we leave him playing the French horn at a relation's house; while she, in her father's home, is supposed to be unnoticed, so much are they all taken up with the rejoicings over the double wedding. It is very probable that when Goldsmith began the story he had no very definite plot concocted; and that it was only when the much-persecuted Vicar had to be restored to happiness, that he found the entanglements surrounding him, and had to make frantic efforts to break through them. But, be that as it may, it is not for the plot that people now read the *Vicar of Wakefield ;* it is not the intricacies of the story that have made it the delight of the world. Surely human nature must be very much the same when this simple description of a quiet English home went straight to the heart of nations in both hemispheres.

And the wonder is that Goldsmith of all men should have produced such a perfect picture of domestic life. What had his own life been but a moving about between garret and tavern, between bachelor's lodgings and clubs? Where had he seen—unless, indeed, he looked back through the mist of years to the scenes of his childhood—all this gentle government, and wise blindness; all this affection, and consideration, and respect? There is as much human nature in the character of the Vicar alone as would have furnished any fifty of the novels of that day, or of this. Who has not been charmed by his sly and quaint humour, by his moral dignity and simple vanities, even by the little secrets he reveals to us of his paternal rule. " ' Ay,' returned I, not knowing well what to think of the matter, 'heaven grant they may be both the better for it this day three months ! ' This was one of those observations I usually made to impress my wife with an opinion of my sagacity ; for if the girls succeeded, then it was a pious wish fulfilled ; but if anything unfortunate ensued, then it might be looked on as a prophecy." We know how Miss Olivia was

answered, when, at her mother's prompting, she set up
for being well skilled in controversy :—
" ' Why, my dear, what controversy can she have
read ? ' cried I.   ' It does not occur to me that I ever
put such books into her hands : you certainly overrate
her merit.'—' Indeed, papa,' replied Olivia, ' she does
not ; I have read a great deal of controversy.   I have
read the disputes between Thwackum and Square ; the
controversy between Robinson Crusoe and Friday, the
savage ; and I am now employed in reading the controversy in Religious Courtship.'—' Very well,' cried
I, ' that's a good girl ; I find you are perfectly qualified
for making converts, and so go help your mother to
make the gooseberry pie.' "

It is with a great gentleness that the good man
reminds his wife and daughters that, after their sudden
loss of fortune, it does not become them to wear much
finery. " The first Sunday, in particular, their behaviour
served to mortify me.   I had desired my girls the pre-
ceding night to be dressed early the next day ; for I
always loved to be at church a good while before the
rest of the congregation.   They punctually obeyed my
directions ; but when we were to assemble in the
morning at breakfast, down came my wife and daughters,
dressed out in all their former splendour ; their hair
plastered up with pomatum, their faces patched to taste,
their trains bundled up in a heap behind, and rustling
at every motion.   I could not help smiling at their
vanity, particularly that of my wife, from whom I
expected more discretion.   In this exigence, therefore,
my only resource was to order my son, with an important air, to call our coach.   The girls were amazed

at the command; but I repeated it with more solemnity
than before. 'Surely, my dear, you jest,' cried my
wife; 'we can walk it perfectly well: we want no
coach to carry us now.'—'You mistake, child,' returned
I, 'we do want a coach; for if we walk to church in
this trim, the very children in the parish will hoot after
us.'—'Indeed,' replied my wife, 'I always imagined
that my Charles was fond of seeing his children neat
and handsome about him.'—'You may be as neat as
you please,' interrupted I, 'and I shall love you the
better for it; but all this is not neatness, but frippery.
These rufflings, and pinkings, and patchings will only
make us hated by all the wives of our neighbours. No,
my children,' continued I, more gravely, 'those gowns
may be altered into something of a plainer cut; for finery
is very unbecoming in us, who want the means of
decency. I do not know whether such flouncing and
shredding is becoming even in the rich, if we consider,
upon a moderate calculation, that the nakedness of the
indigent world might be clothed from the trimmings of
the vain.'

"This remonstrance had the proper effect: they went
with great composure, that very instant, to change their
dress; and the next day I had the satisfaction of finding
my daughters, at their own request, employed in cutting
up their trains into Sunday waistcoats for Dick and
Bill, the two little ones; and, what was still more
satisfactory, the gowns seemed improved by this cur-
tailing." And again when he discovered the two girls
making a wash for their faces:—"My daughters seemed
equally busy with the rest; and I observed them for a
good while cooking something over the fire. I at first

supposed they were assisting their mother, but little
Dick informed me, in a whisper, that they were making
a wash for the face. Washes of all kinds I had a
natural antipathy to; for I knew that, instead of
mending the complexion, they spoil it. I therefore
approached my chair by sly degrees to the fire, and
grasping the poker, as if it wanted mending, seemingly
by accident overturned the whole composition, and it
was too late to begin another."

All this is done with such a light, homely touch,
that one gets familiarly to know these people without
being aware of it. There is no insistance. There is no
dragging you along by the collar; confronting you with
certain figures; and compelling you to look at this and
study that. The artist stands by you, and laughs in
his quiet way; and you are laughing too, when suddenly
you find that human beings have silently come into the
void before you; and you know them for friends; and
even after the vision has faded away, and the beautiful
light and colour and glory of romance-land have
vanished, you cannot forget them. They have become
part of your life; you will take them to the grave
with you.

The story, as every one perceives, has its obvious
blemishes. "There are an hundred faults in this Thing,"
says Goldsmith himself, in the prefixed Advertisement.
But more particularly, in the midst of all the impossi-
bilities taking place in and around the jail, when that
chameleon-like *deus ex machinâ*, Mr. Jenkinson, winds
up the tale in hot haste, Goldsmith pauses to put in a
sort of apology. "Nor can I go on without a reflection,"
he says gravely, " on those accidental meetings, which,

though they happen every day, seldom excite our
surprise but upon some extraordinary occasion.   To
what a fortuitous concurrence do we not owe every
pleasure and convenience of our lives !   How many
seeming accidents must unite before we can be clothed
or fed !   The peasant must be disposed to labour, the
shower must fall, the wind fill the merchant's sail, or
numbers must want the usual supply."   This is Mr.
Thackeray's "simple rogue" appearing again in adult
life.   Certainly, if our supply of food and clothing
depended on such accidents as happened to make the
Vicar's family happy all at once, there would be a good
deal of shivering and starvation in the world.   Moreover it may be admitted that on occasion Goldsmith's
fine instinct deserts him ; and even in describing those
domestic relations which are the charm of the novel, he
blunders into the unnatural.   When Mr. Burchell, for
example, leaves the house in consequence of a quarrel
with Mrs. Primrose, the Vicar questions his daughter as
to whether she had received from that poor gentleman
any testimony of his affection for her.   She replies No ;
but remembers to have heard him remark that he never
knew a woman who could find merit in a man that was
poor.   "Such, my dear," continued the Vicar, "is the
common cant of all the unfortunate or idle.   But I
hope you have been taught to judge properly of such
men, and that it would be even madness to expect
happiness from one who has been so very bad an
economist of his own.   Your mother and I have now
better prospects for you.   The next winter, which you
will probably spend in town, will give you opportunities
of making a more prudent choice."   Now it is not at

all likely that a father, however anxious to have his
daughter well married and settled, would ask her so
delicate a question in open domestic circle, and would
then publicly inform her that she was expected to choose
a husband on her forthcoming visit to town.

Whatever may be said about any particular incident
like this, the atmosphere of the book is true. Goethe, to
whom a German translation of the *Vicar* was read by
Herder some four years after the publication in England,
not only declared it at the time to be one of the best
novels ever written, but again and again throughout his
life reverted to the charm and delight with which he
had made the acquaintance of the English "prose-idyll,"
and took it for granted that it was a real picture of
English life. Despite all the machinery of Mr. Jenkinson's schemes, who could doubt it? Again and again
there are recurrent strokes of such vividness and naturalness that we yield altogether to the necromancer. Look
at this perfect picture—of human emotion and outside
nature—put in in a few sentences. The old clergyman,
after being in search of his daughter, has found her,
and is now—having left her in an inn—returning to his
family and his home. " And now my heart caught new
sensations of pleasure, the nearer I approached that
peaceful mansion. As a bird that had been frighted
from its nest, my affections outwent my haste, and
hovered round my little fireside with all the rapture of
expectation. I called up the many fond things I had to
say, and anticipated the welcome I was to receive. I
already felt my wife's tender embrace, and smiled at
the joy of my little ones. As I walked but slowly, the
night waned apace. The labourers of the day were all

retired to rest ; the lights were out in every cottage ; no
sounds were heard but of the shrilling cock, and the
deep-mouthed watch-dog at hollow distance. I approached my little abode of pleasure, and, before I was
within a furlong of the place, our honest mastiff came
running to welcome me." " *The deep-mouthed watch-dog
at hollow distance ; "*—what more perfect description of
the stillness of night was ever given ?

And then there are other qualities in this delightful
Vicar of Wakefield than merely idyllic tenderness, and
pathos, and sly humour. There is a firm presentation of
the crimes and brutalities of the world. The pure light
that shines within that domestic circle is all the brighter
because of the black outer ring that is here and there
indicated rather than described. How could we ap-
preciate all the simplicities of the good man's household,
but for the rogueries with which they are brought in
contact ? And although we laugh at Moses and his gross
of green spectacles, and the manner in which the Vicar's
wife and daughter are imposed on by Miss Wilhelmina
Skeggs and Lady Blarney, with their lords and ladies
and their tributes to virtue, there is no laughter demanded of us when we find the simplicity and moral
dignity of the Vicar meeting and beating the jeers and
taunts of the abandoned wretches in the prison. This
is really a remarkable episode. The author was under
the obvious temptation to make much comic material
out of the situation ; while another temptation, towards
the goody-goody side, was not far off. But the Vicar
undertakes the duty of reclaiming these castaways
with a modest patience and earnestness in every way in
keeping with his character ; while they, on the other

hand, are not too easily moved to tears of repentance.
His first efforts, it will be remembered, were not too
successful. "Their insensibility excited my highest com-
passion, and blotted my own uneasiness from my mind.
It even appeared a duty incumbent upon me to attempt
to reclaim them. I resolved, therefore, once more to
return, and, in spite of their contempt, to give them my
advice, and conquer them by my perseverance. Going,
therefore, among them again, I informed Mr. Jenkinson
of my design, at which he laughed heartily, but com-
municated it to the rest. The proposal was received
with the greatest good humour, as it promised to afford
a new fund of entertainment to persons who had now
no other resource for mirth but what could be derived
from ridicule or debauchery.

"I therefore read them a portion of the service with a
loud, unaffected voice, and found my audience perfectly
merry upon the occasion. Lewd whispers, groans of
contrition burlesqued, winking and coughing, alternately
excited laughter. However, I continued with my natural
solemnity to read on, sensible that what I did might
mend some, but could itself receive no contamination
from any.

"After reading, I entered upon my exhortation, which
was rather calculated at first to amuse them than to re-
prove. I previously observed, that no other motive but
their welfare could induce me to this ; that I was their
fellow-prisoner, and now got nothing by preaching. I
was sorry, I said, to hear them so very profane ; because
they got nothing by it, but might lose a great deal :
'For be assured, my friends,' cried I,—'for you are my
friends, however the world may disclaim your friendship,

—though you swore twelve thousand oaths in a day, it would not put one penny in your purse. Then what signifies calling every moment upon the devil, and courting his friendship, since you find how scurvily he uses you? He has given you nothing here, you find, but a mouthful of oaths and an empty belly ; and, by the best accounts I have of him, he will give you nothing that's good hereafter.

" ' If used ill in our dealings with one man, we naturally go elsewhere. Were it not worth your while, then, just to try how you may like the usage of another master, who gives you fair promises at least to come to him? Surely, my friends, of all stupidity in the world, his must be the greatest, who, after robbing a house, runs to the thief-takers for protection. And yet, how are you more wise? You are all seeking comfort from one that has already betrayed you, applying to a more malicious being than any thief-taker of them all; for they only decoy and then hang you ; but he decoys and hangs, and, what is worst of all, will not let you loose after the hangman has done.'

" When I had concluded, I received the compliments of my audience, some of whom came and shook me by the hand, swearing that I was a very honest fellow, and that they desired my further acquaintance. I therefore promised to repeat my lecture next day, and actually conceived some hopes of making a reformation here ; for it had ever been my opinion, that no man was past the hour of amendment, every heart lying open to the shafts of reproof, if the archer could but take a proper aim."

His wife and children, naturally dissuading him from an effort which seemed to them only to bring ridicule

upon him, are met by a grave rebuke ; and on the next
morning he descends to the common prison, where, he
says, he found the prisoners very merry, expecting his
arrival, and each prepared to play some gaol-trick on
the Doctor.

"There was one whose trick gave more universal
pleasure than all the rest ; for, observing the manner in
which I had disposed my books on the table before me,
he very dexterously displaced one of them, and put an
obscene jest-book of his own in the place. However, I
took no notice of all that this mischievous group of little
beings could do, but went on, perfectly sensible that what
was ridiculous in my attempt would excite mirth only
the first or second time, while what was serious would
be permanent. My design succeeded, and in less than
six days some were penitent, and all attentive.

" It was now that I applauded my perseverance and
address, at thus giving sensibility to wretches divested
of every moral feeling, and now began to think of doing
them temporal services also, by rendering their situation
somewhat more comfortable. Their time had hitherto
been divided between famine and excess, tumultuous riot
and bitter repining. Their only employment was quarrelling among each other, playing at cribbage, and
cutting tobacco-stoppers. From this last mode of idle
industry I took the hint of setting such as choose to
work at cutting pegs for tobacconists and shoemakers,
the proper wood being bought by a general subscription,
and, when manufactured, sold by my appointment ; so
that each earned something every day—a trifle indeed,
but sufficient to maintain him.

" I did not stop here, but instituted fines for the punish-

H

ment of immorality, and rewards for peculiar industry.
Thus, in less than a fortnight I had formed them into
something social and humane, and had the pleasure of
regarding myself as a legislator who had brought men
from their native ferocity into friendship and obedience."
   Of course, all this about gaols and thieves was calculated to shock the nerves of those who liked their
literature perfumed with rose-water.   Madame Ricco-
boni, to whom Burke had sent the book, wrote to
Garrick, "Le plaidoyer en faveur des voleurs, des
petits larrons, des gens de mauvaises mœurs, est fort
éloigné de me plaire."   Others, no doubt, considered
the introduction of Miss Skeggs and Lady Blarney as
"vastly low."   But the curious thing is that the literary
critics of the day seem to have been altogether silent
about the book—perhaps they were "puzzled" by it,
as Southey has suggested.   Mr. Forster, who took the
trouble to search the periodical literature of the time,
says that, "apart from bald recitals of the plot, not a
word was said in the way of criticism about the book,
either in praise or blame."   The *St. James's Chronicle* did
not condescend to notice its appearance, and the *Monthly
Review* confessed frankly that nothing was to be made
of it.   The better sort of newspapers, as well as the
more dignified reviews, contemptuously left it to the
patronage of *Lloyd's Evening Post*, the *London Chronicle*,
and journals of that class ; which simply informed their
readers that a new novel, called the *Vicar of Wakefield*, had been published, that "the editor is Doctor
Goldsmith, who has affixed his name to an introductory
Advertisement, and that such and such were the incidents of the story."   Even his friends, with the excep-

tion of Burke, did not seem to consider that any remarkable new birth in literature had occurred; and it
is probable that this was a still greater disappointment
to Goldsmith, who was so anxious to be thought well of
at the Club.   However, the public took to the story.
A second edition was published in May; a third in
August.   Goldsmith, it is true, received no pecuniary
gain from this success, for, as we have seen, Johnson
had sold the novel outright to Francis Newbery; but
his name was growing in importance with the booksellers.

There was need that it should, for his increasing
expenses—his fine clothes, his suppers, his whist at
the Devil Tavern—were involving him in deeper
and deeper difficulties.   How was he to extricate himself?—or rather the question that would naturally
occur to Goldsmith was how was he to continue that
hand-to-mouth existence that had its compensations
along with its troubles?   Novels like the *Vicar of
Wakefield* are not written at a moment's notice, even
though any Newbery, judging by results, is willing to
double that £60 which Johnson considered to be a fair
price for the story at the time.   There was the usual
resource of hack-writing; and, no doubt, Goldsmith was
compelled to fall back on that, if only to keep the elder
Newbery, in whose debt he was, in a good humour.   But
the author of the *Vicar of Wakefield* may be excused if
he looked round to see if there was not some more
profitable work for him to turn his hand to.   It was at
this time that he began to think of writing a comedy.

CHAPTER XII.

THE GOOD-NATURED MAN.

AMID much miscellaneous work, mostly of the compilation order, the play of the *Good-natured Man* began to assume concrete form; insomuch that Johnson, always the friend of this erratic Irishman, had promised to write a Prologue for it. It is with regard to this Prologue that Boswell tells a foolish and untrustworthy story about Goldsmith. Dr. Johnson had recently been honoured by an interview with his Sovereign; and the members of the Club were in the habit of flattering him by begging for a repetition of his account of that famous event. On one occasion, during this recital, Boswell relates, Goldsmith " remained unmoved upon a sofa at some distance, affecting not to join in the least in the eager curiosity of the company. He assigned as a reason for his gloom and seeming inattention that he apprehended Johnson had relinquished his purpose of furnishing him with a Prologue to his play, with the hopes of which he had been flattered; but it was strongly suspected that he was fretting with chagrin and envy at the singular honour Doctor Johnson had lately enjoyed. At length the frankness and simplicity of his natural character prevailed. He sprang from the sofa, advanced to Johnson, and, in a kind of flutter, from imagining himself in the situation which he had just been hearing described, exclaimed, ' Well, you acquitted yourself in this conversation better than I should have done ; for I should have bowed and stammered through the whole of it.' " It is obvious enough that the only part of this anecdote which is quite worthy of credence is the actual phrase used by Goldsmith, which is full of his customary generosity and self-depreciation. All those " suspicions " of his envy of his friend may safely be discarded, for they are mere guesswork ; even though it might have been natural enough for a man like Goldsmith, conscious of his singular and original genius, to measure himself against Johnson, who was merely a man of keen perception and shrewd reasoning, and to compare the deference paid to Johnson with the scant courtesy shown to himself.

As a matter of fact, the Prologue was written by Dr. Johnson ; and the now complete comedy was, after some little arrangement of personal differences between Goldsmith and Garrick, very kindly undertaken by Reynolds, submitted for Garrick's approval. But nothing came of Reynolds's intervention. Perhaps Goldsmith resented Garrick's airs of patronage towards a poor devil of an author ; perhaps Garrick was surprised by the manner in which well-intentioned criticisms were taken ; at all events, after a good deal of shilly-shallying, the play was taken out of Garrick's hands. Fortunately, a project was just at this moment on foot for starting the rival theatre in Covent Garden, under the management of George Colman; and to Colman Goldsmith's play was forthwith consigned. The play was accepted; but it was a long time before it was produced; and in that interval it may fairly be presumed the *res angusta domi* of Goldsmith did not become any more free and generous than before. It was in this interval that the elder Newbery died; Goldsmith had one patron the less. Another patron who offered himself was civilly bowed to the door. This is an incident in Goldsmith's career which, like his interview with the Earl of Northumberland, should ever be remembered in his honour. The Government of the day were desirous of enlisting on their behalf the services of writers of somewhat better position than the mere libellers whose pens were the slaves of any-body's purse; and a Mr. Scott, a chaplain of Lord Sandwich, appears to have imagined that it would be be worth while to buy Goldsmith. He applied to Goldsmith in due course; and this is an account of the interview. "I found him in a miserable set of chambers in the Temple. I told him my authority; I told him I was empowered to pay most liberally for his exertions; and, would you believe it! he was so absurd as to say, 'I can earn as much as will supply my wants without writing for any party; the assistance you offer is there-fore unnecessary to me.' And I left him in his garret." Needy as he was, Goldsmith had too much self-respect to become a paid libeller and cutthroat of public reputations.

On the evening of Friday, the 29th of January, 1768, when Goldsmith had now reached the age of forty, the comedy of *The Good-natured Man* was produced at

Covent Garden Theatre. The Prologue had, according to promise, been written by Johnson; and a very singular prologue it was. Even Boswell was struck by the odd contrast between this sonorous piece of melancholy and the fun that was to follow. "The first lines of this Prologue," he conscientiously remarks, "are strongly characteristical of the dismal gloom of his mind; which, in his case, as in the case of all who are distressed with the same malady of imagination, transfers to others its own feelings. Who could suppose it was to introduce a comedy, when Mr. Bensley solemnly began—

> " ' Pressed with the load of life, the weary mind
> Surveys the general toil of humankind ' ?

But this dark ground might make Goldsmith's humour shine the more.'' When we come to the comedy itself, we find but little bright humour in the opening passages. The author is obviously timid, anxious, and constrained. There is nothing of the brisk, confident vivacity with which *She Stoops to Conquer* opens. The novice does not yet understand the art of making his characters explain themselves; and accordingly the benevolent uncle and honest Jarvis indulge in a conversation which, laboriously descriptive of the character of young Honeywood, is spoken " at " the audience. With the entrance of young Honeywood himself, Goldsmith endeavours to become a little more sprightly; but there is still anxiety hanging over him, and the epigrams are little more than merely formal antitheses.

" *Jarvis.* This bill from your tailor ; this from your mercer ; and this from the little broker in Crooked Lane. He says he has been at a great deal of trouble to get back the money you borrowed.

Hon. That I don't know ; but I'm sure we were at a great deal of trouble in getting him to lend it.

Jar. He has lost all patience.

Hon. Then he has lost a very good thing.

Jar. There's that ten guineas you were sending to the poor gentleman and his children in the Fleet. I believe that would stop his mouth for a while at least.

Hon. Ay, Jarvis, but what will fill their mouths in the mean time ? "

This young Honeywood, the hero of the play, is, and remains throughout, a somewhat ghostly personage. He has attributes ; but no flesh or blood. There is much more substance in the next character introduced—the inimitable Croaker, who revels in evil forebodings and drinks deep of the luxury of woe. These are the two chief characters ; but then a play must have a plot. And perhaps it would not be fair, so far as the plot is concerned, to judge of *The Good-natured Man* merely as a literary production. Intricacies that seem tedious and puzzling on paper appear to be clear enough on the stage : it is much more easy to remember the history and circumstances of a person whom we see before us, than to attach these to a mere name—especially as the name is sure to be clipped down from *Honeywood* to *Hon.* and from *Leontine* to *Leon.* However, it is in the midst of all the cross-purposes of the lovers that we once more come upon our old friend Beau Tibbs—though Mr. Tibbs is now in much better circumstances, and has been re-named by his creator Jack Lofty. Garrick had objected to the introduction of Jack, on the ground that he was only a distraction. But Goldsmith, whether

in writing a novel or a play, was more anxious to represent human nature than to prune a plot, and paid
but little respect to the unities, if only he could
arouse our interest. And who is not delighted with
this Jack Lofty and his " duchessy " talk—his airs of
patronage, his mysterious hints, his gay familiarity with
the great, his audacious lying ?

"*Lofty.* Waller ? Waller ? Is he of the house ?
Mrs. Croaker. The modern poet of that name, sir.
Lof. Oh, a modern ! We men of business despise the
moderns ; and as for the ancients, we have no time to read
them. Poetry is a pretty thing enough for our wives and
daughters ; but not for us. Why now, here I stand that
know nothing of books. I say, madam, I know nothing of
books ; and yet, I believe, upon a land-carriage fishery, a
stamp act, or a jag-hire, I can talk my two hours without
feeling the want of them.
Mrs. Cro. The world is no stranger to Mr. Lofty's eminence
in every capacity.
Lof. I vow to gad, madam, you make me blush. I'm
nothing, nothing, nothing in the world ; a mere obscure
gentleman. To be sure, indeed, one or two of the present
ministers are pleased to represent me as a formidable man.
I know they are pleased to bespatter me at all their little
dirty levees. Yet, upon my soul, I wonder what they see
in me to treat me so ! Measures, not men, have always been
my mark ; and I vow, by all that's honourable, my resentment has never done the men, as mere men, any manner of
harm—that is, as mere men.
Mrs. Cro. What importance, and yet what modesty !
Lof. Oh, if you talk of modesty, madam, there, I own, I'm
accessible to praise : modesty is my foible : it was so the
Duke of Brentford used to say of me. ' I love Jack Lofty,'
he used to say : ' no man has a finer knowledge of things ;
quite a man of information ; and when he speaks upon his

legs, by the Lord he's prodigious, he scouts them ; and yet all
men have their faults ; too much modesty is his,' says his
grace.

Mrs. Cro. And yet, I dare say, you don't want assurance
when you come to solicit for your friends.

Lof. Oh, there indeed I'm in bronze. Apropos ! I have
just been mentioning Miss Richland's case to a certain personage ; we must name no names.   When I ask, I am not to
be put off, madam.   No, no, I take my friend by the button.
A fine girl, sir ; great justice in her case.   A friend of mine
—borough interest—business must be done, Mr. Secretary.—
I say, Mr. Secretary, her business must be done, sir.   That's
my way, madam.

Mrs. Cro. Bless me ! you said all this to the Secretary of
State, did you ?

Lof. I did not say the Secretary, did I ? Well, curse it,
since you have found me out, I will not deny it.   It was to
the Secretary."

Strangely enough, what may now seem to some of us
the very best scene in the *Good-natured Man*—the scene,
that is, in which young Honeywood, suddenly finding
Miss Richland without, is compelled to dress up the two
bailiffs in possession of his house and introduce them to
her as gentlemen friends—was very nearly damning the
play on the first night of its production.   The pit was
of opinion that it was "low ; " and subsequently the
critics took up the cry, and professed themselves to be
so deeply shocked by the vulgar humours of the bailiffs
that Goldsmith had to cut them out.   But on the opening night the anxious author, who had been rendered
nearly distracted by the cries and hisses produced by
this scene, was somewhat reassured when the audience
began to laugh again over the tribulations of Mr.
Croaker.   To the actor who played the part he expressed

his warm gratitude when the piece was over; assuring
him that he had exceeded his own conception of the
character, and that "the fine comic richness of his
colouring made it almost appear as new to him as to
any other person in the house."

The new play had been on the whole favourably
received; and, when Goldsmith went along afterwards
to the Club, his companions were doubtless not at all
surprised to find him in good spirits. He was even
merrier than usual; and consented to sing his favourite
ballad about the Old Woman tossed in a Blanket. But
those hisses and cries were still rankling in his memory;
and he himself subsequently confessed that he was
"suffering horrid tortures." Nay, when the other members of the Club had gone, leaving him and Johnson
together, he "burst out a-crying, and even swore by ——
that he would never write again." When Goldsmith
told this story in after-days, Johnson was naturally
astonished; perhaps—himself not suffering much from
an excessive sensitiveness—he may have attributed that
little burst of hysterical emotion to the excitement of
the evening increased by a glass or two of punch, and
determined therefore never to mention it. "All which,
Doctor," he said, "I thought had been a secret between
you and me; and I am sure I would not have said anything about it for the world." Indeed there was little
to cry over, either in the first reception of the piece or
in its subsequent fate. With the offending bailiffs cut
out, the comedy would seem to have been very fairly
successful. The proceeds of three of the evenings were
Goldsmith's payment; and in this manner he received
£400. Then Griffin published the play; and from this

source Goldsmith received an additional £100 ; so that altogether he was very well paid for his work.   Moreover he had appealed against the judgment of the pit and the dramatic critics, by printing in the published edition the bailiff scene which had been removed from the stage ; and the *Monthly Review* was so extremely kind as to say that " the bailiff and his blackguard follower appeared intolerable on the stage, yet we are not disgusted with them in the perusal."   Perhaps we have grown less scrupulous since then ; but at all events it would be difficult for anybody nowadays to find anything but good-natured fun in that famous scene.   There is an occasional "damn," it is true ; but then English officers have always been permitted that little playfulness, and these two gentlemen were supposed to " serve in the Fleet ; " while if they had been particularly refined in their speech and manner, how could the author have aroused Miss Richland's suspicions ?   It is possible that the two actors who played the bailiff and his follower may have introduced some vulgar " gag" into their parts ; but there is no warranty for anything of the kind in the play as we now read it.

CHAPTER XIII.

THE appearance of the *Good-natured Man* ushered in a halcyon period in Goldsmith's life. The *Traveller* and the *Vicar* had gained for him only reputation : this new comedy put £500 in his pocket. Of course that was too big a sum for Goldsmith to have about him long. Four-fifths of it he immediately expended on the purchase and decoration of a set of chambers in Brick Court, Middle Temple ; with the remainder he appears to have begun a series of entertainments in this new abode, which were perhaps more remarkable for their mirth than their decorum. There was no sort of frolic in which Goldsmith would not indulge for the amusement of his guests ; he would sing them songs ; he would throw his wig to the ceiling ; he would dance a minuet. And then they had cards, forfeits, blind-man's-buff, until Mr. Blackstone, then engaged on his *Commentaries* in the rooms below, was driven nearly mad by the uproar. These parties would seem to have been of a most nondescript character—chance gatherings of any obscure authors or actors whom he happened to meet ; but from time to time there were more formal enter-

tainments, at which Johnson, Percy, and similar distinguished persons were present. Moreover, Dr. Goldsmith
himself was much asked out to dinner too; and so, not
content with the "Tyrian bloom, satin grain and garter,
blue-silk breeches,'' which Mr. Filby had provided for
the evening of the production of the comedy, he now
had another suit "lined with silk, and gold buttons,"
that he might appear in proper guise. Then he had his
airs of consequence too. This was his answer to an
invitation from Kelly, who was his rival of the hour :
" I would with pleasure accept your kind invitation, but
to tell you the truth, my dear boy, my *Traveller* has
found me a home in so many places, that I am engaged,
I believe, three days. Let me see. To-day I dine with
Edmund Burke, to-morrow with Dr. Nugent, and the
next day with Topham Beauclerc ; but I'll tell you
what I'll do for you, I'll dine with you on Saturday."
Kelly told this story as against Goldsmith ; but surely
there is not so much ostentation in the reply. Directly
after *Tristram Shandy* was published, Sterne found
himself fourteen deep in dinner engagements : why
should not the author of the *Traveller* and the *Vicar*
and the *Good-natured Man* have his engagements also ?
And perhaps it was but right that Mr. Kelly, who was
after all only a critic and scribbler, though he had
written a play which was for the moment enjoying an
undeserved popularity, should be given to understand
that Dr. Goldsmith was not to be asked to a hole-
and-corner chop at a moment's notice. To-day he dines
with Mr. Burke ; to-morrow with Dr. Nugent ; the
day after with Mr. Beauclerc. If you wish to have the
honour of his company, you may choose a day after

that; and then, with his new wig, with his coat of
Tyrian bloom and blue silk breeches, with a smart
sword at his side, his gold-headed cane in his hand,
and his hat under his elbow, he will present himself
in due course.   Dr. Goldsmith is announced, and
makes his grave bow : this is the man of genius about
whom all the town is talking ; the friend of Burke, of
Reynolds, of Johnson, of Hogarth ; this is not the ragged
Irishman who was some time ago earning a crust by
running errands for an apothecary.

Goldsmith's grand airs, however, were assumed but
seldom ; and they never imposed on anybody.   His
acquaintances treated him with a familiarity which
testified rather to his good-nature than to their good
taste.   Now and again, indeed, he was prompted to
resent this familiarity ; but the effort was not successful.
In the " high jinks " to which he good-humouredly resorted for the entertainment of his guests he permitted
a freedom which it was afterwards not very easy to
discard ; and as he was always ready to make a butt of
himself for the amusement of his friends and acquaintances, it came to be recognised that anybody was allowed
to play off a joke on " Goldy."   The jokes, such of them
as have been put on record, are of the poorest sort.   The
horse-collar is never far off.   One gladly turns from
these dismal humours of the tavern and the club to the
picture of Goldsmith's enjoying what he called a " Shoemaker's Holiday " in the company of one or two chosen
intimates.   Goldsmith, baited and bothered by the wits
of a public-house, became a different being when he had
assumed the guidance of a small party of chosen friends
bent on having a day's frugal pleasure.   We are indebted

to one Cooke, a neighbour of Goldsmith's in the Temple,
not only for a most interesting description of one of
those shoemaker's holidays, but also for the knowledge
that Goldsmith had even now begun writing the *Deserted
Village*, which was not published till 1770, two years
later. Goldsmith, though he could turn out plenty of
manufactured stuff for the booksellers, worked slowly
at the special story or poem with which he meant to
"strike for honest fame." This Mr. Cooke, calling on
him one morning, discovered that Goldsmith had that
day written these ten lines of the *Deserted Village* :—

> " Dear lovely bowers of innocence and ease,
> Seats of my youth, when every sport could please,
> How often have I loitered o'er thy green,
> Where humble happiness endeared each scene !
> How often have I paused on every charm,
> The sheltered cot, the cultivated farm,
> The never-failing brook, the busy mill,
> The decent church, that topt the neighbouring hill,
> The hawthorn bush, with seats beneath the shade,
> For talking age and whispering lovers made ! "

"Come," said he, "let me tell you this is no bad
morning's work; and now, my dear boy, if you are
not better engaged, I should be glad to enjoy a shoemaker's holiday with you." "A shoemaker's holiday,"
continues the writer of these reminiscences, "was a
day of great festivity to poor Goldsmith, and was spent
in the following innocent manner. Three or four of
his intimate friends rendezvoused at his chambers to
breakfast about ten o'clock in the morning; at eleven
they proceeded by the City Road and through the fields

to Highbury Barn to dinner ; about six o'clock in the
evening they adjourned to White Conduit House to drink
tea ; and concluded by supping at the Grecian or Temple
Exchange coffee-house or at the Globe in Fleet Street.
There was a very good ordinary of two dishes and pastry
kept at Highbury Barn about this time at tenpence per
head, including a penny to the waiter ; and the company
generally consisted of literary characters, a few Templars,
and some citizens who had left off trade. The whole
expenses of the day's fete never exceeded a crown, and
oftener were from three-and-sixpence to four shillings ;
for which the party obtained good air and exercise,
good living, the example of simple manners, and good
conversation."

It would have been well indeed for Goldsmith had he
been possessed of sufficient strength of character to
remain satisfied with these simple pleasures, and to
have lived the quiet and modest life of a man of letters
on such income as he could derive from the best work
he could produce. But it is this same Mr. Cooke who
gives decisive testimony as to Goldsmith's increasing
desire to "shine" by imitating the expenditure of the
great; the natural consequence of which was that he
only plunged himself into a morass of debt, advances,
contracts for hack-work, and misery. "His debts rendered him at times so melancholy and dejected, that I
am sure he felt himself a very unhappy man." Perhaps
it was with some sudden resolve to flee from temptation,
and grapple with the difficulties that beset him, that he,
in conjunction with another Temple neighbour, Mr.
Bott, rented a cottage some eight miles down the Edgware
Road ; and here he set to work on the *History of Rome*,

I

which he was writing for Davies. Apart from this hack-work, now rendered necessary by his debt, it is probable that one strong inducement leading him to this occasional seclusion was the progress he might be able to make with the *Deserted Village*. Amid all his town gaieties and country excursions, amid his dinners and suppers and dances, his borrowings, and contracts, and the hurried literary produce of the moment, he never forgot what was due to his reputation as an English poet. The journalistic bullies of the day might vent their spleen and envy on him; his best friends might smile at his conversational failures; the wits of the tavern might put up the horse-collar as before; but at least he had the consolation of his art. No one better knew than himself the value of those finished and musical lines he was gradually adding to the beautiful poem, the grace, and sweetness, and tender, pathetic charm of which make it one of the literary treasures of the English people.

The sorrows of debt were not Goldsmith's only trouble at this time. For some reason or other he seems to have become the especial object of spiteful attack on the part of the literary cut-throats of the day. And Goldsmith, though he might listen with respect to the wise advice of Johnson on such matters, was never able to cultivate Johnson's habit of absolute indifference to anything that might be said or sung of him. " The Kenricks, Campbells, MacNicols, and Hendersons," says Lord Macaulay—speaking of Johnson, " did their best to annoy him, in the hope that he would give them importance by answering them. But the reader will in vain search his works for any allusion to Kenrick or

Campbell, to MacNicol or Henderson.   One Scotchman, bent on vindicating the fame of Scotch learning,
defied him to the combat in a detestable Latin hexa-
meter—

> ' Maxime, si tu vis, cupio contendere tecum.'

But Johnson took no notice of the challenge.   He had
learned, both from his own observation and from literary
history, in which he was deeply read, that the place of
books in the public estimation is fixed, not by what is
written about them, but by what is written in them;
and that an author whose works are likely to live, is
very unwise if he stoops to wrangle with detractors
whose works are certain to die.   He always maintained
that fame was a shuttlecock which could be kept up only
by being beaten back, as well as beaten forward, and
which would soon fall if there were only one battledore.
No saying was oftener in his mouth than that fine
apophthegm of Bentley, that no man was ever written
down but by himself."

It was not given to Goldsmith to feel "like the
Monument" on any occasion whatsoever.   He was
anxious to have the esteem of his friends; he was
sensitive to a degree; denunciation or malice, be-
gotten of envy that Johnson would have passed un-
heeded, wounded him to the quick.   "The insults to
which he had to submit," Thackeray wrote with a quick
and warm sympathy, "are shocking to read of—slander,
contumely, vulgar satire, brutal malignity perverting
his commonest motives and actions : he had his share
of these, and one's anger is roused at reading of them,
as it is at seeing a woman insulted or a child assaulted,

at the notion that a creature so very gentle, and weak, and full of love should have had to suffer so." Goldsmith's revenge, his defence of himself, his appeal to the public, were the *Traveller*, the *Vicar of Wakefield*, the *Deserted Village ;* but these came at long intervals ; and in the meantime he had to bear with the anonymous malignity that pursued him as best he might. No doubt, when Burke was entertaining him at dinner ; and when Johnson was openly deferring to him in conversation at the Club ; and when Reynolds was painting his portrait, he could afford to forget Mr. Kenrick and the rest of the libelling clan.

The occasions on which Johnson deferred to Goldsmith in conversation were no doubt few ; but at all events the bludgeon of the great Cham would appear to have come down less frequently on "honest Goldy" than on the other members of that famous coterie. It could come down heavily enough. "Sir," said an incautious person, "drinking drives away care, and makes us forget whatever is disagreeable. Would not you allow a man to drink for that reason ?" "Yes, sir," was the reply, "if he sat next *you.*" Johnson, however, was considerate towards Goldsmith, partly because of his affection for him, and partly because he saw under what disadvantages Goldsmith entered the lists. For one thing, the conversation of those evenings would seem to have drifted continually into the mere definition of phrases. Now Johnson had spent years of his life, during the compilation of his Dictionary, in doing nothing else but defining ; and, whenever the dispute took a phraseological turn, he had it all his own way. Goldsmith, on the other hand, was apt to become confused in his eager self-consciousness. " Goldsmith," said Johnson to Boswell, " should not be for ever attempting to shine in conversation ; he has not temper for it, he is so much mortified when he fails. . . When he contends, if he gets the better, it is a very little addition to a man of his literary reputation : if he does not get the better, he is miserably vexed." Boswell, nevertheless, admits that Goldsmith was " often very fortunate in his witty contests, even when he entered the lists with Johnson himself," and goes on to tell how Goldsmith, relating the fable of the little fishes who petitioned Jupiter, and perceiving that Johnson was laughing at him, immediately said, " Why, Dr. Johnson, this is not so easy as you seem to think ; for if you were to make little fishes talk, they would talk like WHALES." Who but Goldsmith would have dared to play jokes on the sage ? At supper they have rumps and kidneys. The sage expresses his approval of " the pretty little things ; " but profoundly observes that one must eat a good many of them before being satisfied. " Ay, but how many of them," asks Goldsmith, " would reach to the moon ? " The sage professes his ignorance ; and, indeed, remarks that that would exceed even Goldsmith's calculations ; when the practical joker observes, " Why, *one*, sir, if it were long enough." Johnson was completely beaten on this occasion. " Well, sir, I have deserved it. I should not have provoked so foolish an answer by so foolish a question."

It was Johnson himself, moreover, who told the story of Goldsmith and himself being in Poets' Corner ; of his saying to Goldsmith

" Forsitan et nostrum nomen miscebitur istis,"

and of Goldsmith subsequently repeating the quotation
when, having walked towards Fleet Street, they were
confronted by the heads on Temple Bar. Even when
Goldsmith was opinionated and wrong, Johnson's con-
tradiction was in a manner gentle. "If you put a tub
full of blood into a stable, the horses are like to go
mad," observed Goldsmith. "I doubt that," was Johnson's reply. "Nay, sir, it is a fact well authenticated."
Here Thrale interposed to suggest that Goldsmith should
have the experiment tried in the stable; but Johnson
merely said that, if Goldsmith began making these experiments, he would never get his book written at all.
Occasionally, of course, Goldsmith was tossed and gored
just like another. "But, sir," he had ventured to say,
in opposition to Johnson, "when people live together
who have something as to which they disagree, and
which they want to shun, they will be in the situation
mentioned in the story of Bluebeard, 'You may look
into all the chambers but one.' But we should have the
greatest inclination to look into that chamber, to talk
of that subject." Here, according to Boswell, Johnson
answered in a loud voice, "Sir, I am not saying that *you*
could live in friendship with a man from whom you differ
as to one point; I am only saying that *I* could do it."
But then again he could easily obtain pardon from the
gentle Goldsmith for any occasional rudeness. One
evening they had a sharp passage of arms at dinner;
and thereafter the company adjourned to the Club, where
Goldsmith sate silent and depressed. "Johnson perceived this," says Boswell, "and said aside to some of
us, 'I'll make Goldsmith forgive me'; and then called to
him in a loud voice, 'Dr. Goldsmith, something passed

to-day where you and I dined : I ask your pardon.'
Goldsmith answered placidly, 'It must be much from
you, sir, that I take ill.'   And so at once the difference
was over, and they were on as easy terms as ever, and
Goldsmith rattled away as usual." For the rest, Johnson
was the constant and doughty champion of Goldsmith
as a man of letters.   He would suffer no one to doubt
the power and versatility of that genius which he had
been amongst the first to recognise and encourage.
" Whether, indeed, we take him as a poet, as a comic
writer, or as an historian," he announced to an assemblage of distinguished persons met together at dinner at
Mr. Beauclerc's, " *he stands in the first class.*" And there
was no one living who dared dispute the verdict—at
least in Johnson's hearing.

CHAPTER XIV.

THE DESERTED VILLAGE.

But it is time to return to the literary performances that gained for this uncouth Irishman so great an amount of consideration from the first men of his time. The engagement with Griffin about the *History of Animated Nature* was made at the beginning of 1769. The work was to occupy eight volumes; and Dr. Goldsmith was to receive eight hundred guineas for the complete copyright. Whether the undertaking was originally a suggestion of Griffin's, or of Goldsmith's own, does not appear. If it was the author's, it was probably only the first means that occurred to him of getting another advance; and that advance—£500 on account —he did actually get. But if it was the suggestion of the publisher, Griffin must have been a bold man. A writer whose acquaintance with animated nature was such as to allow him to make the "insidious tiger" a denizen of the backwoods of Canada,[1] was not a very safe authority. But perhaps Griffin had consulted Johnson before making this bargain; and we know that Johnson, though continually remarking on Goldsmith's

[1] See *Citizen of the World*, Letter XVII.

extraordinary ignorance of facts, was of opinion that the *History of Animated Nature* would be "as entertaining as a Persian tale." However, Goldsmith—no doubt after he had spent the five hundred guineas—tackled the work in earnest. When Boswell subsequently went out to call on him at another rural retreat he had taken on the Edgware Road, Boswell and Mickle, the translator of the *Lusiad*, found Goldsmith from home; "but, having a curiosity to see his apartment, we went in and found curious scraps of descriptions of animals scrawled upon the wall with a black-lead pencil." Meanwhile, this *Animated Nature* being in hand, the *Roman History* was published, and was very well received by the critics and by the public. "Goldsmith's abridgment," Johnson declared, "is better than that of Lucius Florus or Eutropius; and I will venture to say that if you compare him with Vertot, in the same places of the *Roman History*, you will find that he excels Vertot. Sir, he has the art of compiling, and of saying everything he has to say in a pleasing manner."

So thought the booksellers too; and the success of the *Roman History* only involved him in fresh projects of compilation. By an offer of £500 Davies induced him to lay aside for the moment the *Animated Nature* and begin "An History of England, from the Birth of the British Empire to the death of George the Second, in four volumes octavo." He also about this time undertook to write a Life of Thomas Parnell. Here, indeed, was plenty of work, and work promising good pay; but the depressing thing is that Goldsmith should have been the man who had to do it. He may have done it better than any one else could have done—indeed, looking over

the results of all that drudgery, we recognise now the
happy turns of expression which were never long absent
from Goldsmith's prose-writing—but the world could
well afford to sacrifice all the task-work thus got through
for another poem like the *Deserted Village* or the *Traveller.*
Perhaps Goldsmith considered he was making a fair com-
promise when, for the sake of his reputation, he devoted
a certain portion of his time to his poetical work, and
then, to have money for fine clothes and high jinks, gave
the rest to the booksellers.   One critic, on the appearance of the *Roman History,* referred to the *Traveller,*
and remarked that it was a pity that the "author of one
of the best poems that has appeared since those of Mr.
Pope, should not apply wholly to works of imagination."
We may echo that regret now ; but Goldsmith would at
the time have no doubt replied that, if he had trusted to
his poems, he would never have been able to pay £400
for chambers in the Temple.   In fact he said as much
to Lord Lisburn at one of the Academy dinners : "I
cannot afford to court the draggle-tail muses, my Lord ;
they would let me starve ; but by my other labours I
can make shift to eat, and drink, and have good clothes."
And there is little use in our regretting now that Goldsmith was not cast in a more heroic mould ; we have to
take him as he is ; and be grateful for what he has
left us.

It is a grateful relief to turn from these booksellers'
contracts and forced labours to the sweet clear note
of singing that one finds in the *Deserted Village.*
This poem, after having been repeatedly announced and
as often withdrawn for further revision, was at last
published on the 26th of May, 1770, when Goldsmith

was in his forty-second year. The leading idea of it
he had already thrown out in certain lines in the
Traveller :—

> " Have we not seen, round Britain's peopled shore,
>   Her useful sons exchanged for useless ore ?
>   Seen all her triumphs but destruction haste,
>   Like flaring tapers brightening as they waste ?
>   Seen opulence, her grandeur to maintain,
>   Lead stern depopulation in her train,
>   And over fields where scattered hamlets rose
>   In barren solitary pomp repose ?
>   Have we not seen at pleasure's lordly call
>   The smiling long-frequented village fall ?
>   Beheld the duteous son, the sire decayed,
>   The modest matron, and the blushing maid,
>   Forced from their homes, a melancholy train,
>   To traverse climes beyond the western main ;
>   Where wild Oswego spreads her swamps around,
>   And Niagara stuns with thundering sound ? "

—and elsewhere, in recorded conversations of his, we
find that he had somehow got it into his head that the
accumulation of wealth in a country was the parent of
all evils, including depopulation. We need not stay
here to discuss Goldsmith's position as a political economist ; even although Johnson seems to sanction his
theory in the four lines he contributed to the end of the
poem. Nor is it worth while returning to that objection
of Lord Macaulay's which has already been mentioned
in these pages, further than to repeat that the poor Irish
village in which Goldsmith was brought up, no doubt
looked to him as charming as any Auburn, when he
regarded it through the softening and beautifying mist

of years. It is enough that the abandonment by a
number of poor people of the homes in which they and
theirs have lived their lives, is one of the most pathetic
facts in our civilisation ; and that out of the various
circumstances surrounding this forced migration Goldsmith has made one of the most graceful and touching
poems in the English language. It is clear bird-singing ;
but there is a pathetic note in it. That imaginary
ramble through the Lissoy that is far away has recalled
more than his boyish sports ; it has made him look back
over his own life—the life of an exile.

> " I still had hopes, my latest hours to crown,
>   Amidst these humble bowers to lay me down ;
>   To husband out life's taper at the close,
>   And keep the flame from wasting by repose :
>   I still had hopes, for pride attends us still,
>   Amidst the swains to show my book-learned skill,
>   Around my fire an evening group to draw,
>   And tell of all I felt, and all I saw ;
>   And, as a hare whom hounds and horns pursue
>   Pants to the place from whence at first he flew,
>   I still had hopes, my long vexations past,
>   Here to return—and die at home at last."

Who can doubt that it was of Lissoy he was thinking ?
Sir Walter Scott, writing a generation ago, said that
" the church which tops the neighbouring hill," the
mill and the brook were still to be seen in the Irish
village ; and that even

> " The hawthorn bush with seats beneath the shade
>   For talking age and whispering lovers made,"

had been identified by the indefatigable tourist, and
was of course being cut to pieces to make souvenirs.
But indeed it is of little consequence whether we say
that Auburn is an English village, or insist that it is
only Lissoy idealised, as long as the thing is true in
itself.   And we know that this is true : it is not that
one sees the place as a picture, but that one seems to
be breathing its very atmosphere, and listening to
the various cries that thrill the " hollow silence."

" Sweet was the sound, when oft at evening's close
  Up yonder hill the village murmur rose.
  There, as I past with careless steps and slow,
  The mingling notes came softened from below ;
  The swain responsive as the milk-maid sung,
  The sober herd that lowed to meet their young,
  The noisy geese that gabbled o'er the pool,
  The playful children just let loose from school,
  The watch-dog's voice that bayed the whispering wind,
  And the loud laugh that spake the vacant mind."

Nor is it any romantic and impossible peasantry that
is gradually brought before us.   There are no Norvals in
Lissoy.   There is the old woman— Catherine Geraghty,
they say, was her name—who gathered cresses in the
ditches near her cabin.   There is the village preacher
whom Mrs. Hodson, Goldsmith's sister, took to be a
portrait of their father ; but whom others have identified
as Henry Goldsmith, and even as the uncle Contarine :
they may all have contributed.   And then comes Paddy
Byrne.   Amid all the pensive tenderness of the poem
this description of the schoolmaster, with its strokes of
demure humour, is introduced with delightful effect.

" Beside yon straggling fence that skirts the way,
With blossom'd furze unprofitably gay,
There, in his noisy mansion, skilled to rule,
The village master taught his little school.
A man severe he was, and stern to view ;
I knew him well, and every truant knew :
Well had the boding tremblers learned to trace
The day's disasters in his morning face ;
Full well they laughed with counterfeited glee
At all his jokes, for many a joke had he ;
Full well the busy whisper circling round
Conveyed the dismal tidings when he frowned.
Yet he was kind, or, if severe in aught,
The love he bore to learning was in fault ;
The village all declared how much he knew :
'Twas certain he could write, and cipher too :
Lands he could measure, terms and tides presage,
And e'en the story ran that he could gauge :
In arguing, too, the parson owned his skill ;
For e'en though vanquished, he could argue still ;
While words of learned length and thundering sound
Amazed the gazing rustics ranged around ;
And still they gazed, and still the wonder grew
That one small head could carry all he knew."

All this is so simple and natural that we cannot fail to
believe in the reality of Auburn, or Lissoy, or whatever
the village may be supposed to be. We visit the clergyman's cheerful fireside ; and look in on the noisy school ;
and sit in the evening in the ale-house to listen to the
profound politics talked there. But the crisis comes.
Auburn *delenda est*. Here, no doubt, occurs the least
probable part of the poem. Poverty of soil is a common
cause of emigration ; land that produces oats (when
it can produce oats at all) three-fourths mixed with
weeds, and hay chiefly consisting of rushes, naturally

discharges its surplus population as families increase ; and though the wrench of parting is painful enough, the usual result is a change from starvation to competence. It more rarely happens that a district of peace and plenty, such as Auburn was supposed to see around it, is depopulated to add to a great man's estate.

> " The man of wealth and pride
> Takes up a space that many poor supplied ;
> Space for his lake, his park's extended bounds,
> Space for his horses, equipage, and hounds :
> ✿   ✿   ✿   ✿   ✿   ✿
> His seat, where solitary sports are seen,
> Indignant spurns the cottage from the green : "

—and so forth. This seldom happens ; but it does happen ; and it has happened, in our own day, in England. It is within the last twenty years that an English landlord, having faith in his riches, bade a village be removed and cast elsewhere, so that it should no longer be visible from his windows : and it was forth· with removed. But any solitary instance like this is not sufficient to support the theory that wealth and luxury are inimical to the existence of a hardy peasantry ; and so we must admit, after all, that it is poetical exigency rather than political economy that has decreed the destruction of the loveliest village of the plain. Where, asks the poet, are the driven poor to find refuge. when even the fenceless commons are seized upon and divided by the rich ?   In the great cities ?—

> " To see profusion that he must not share ;
> To see ten thousand baneful arts combined
> To pamper luxury and thin mankind."

It is in this description of a life in cities that there
occurs an often-quoted passage, which has in it one of
the most perfect lines in English poetry :—

> " Ah, turn thine eyes
> Where the poor houseless shivering female lies.
> She once, perhaps, in village plenty blest,
> Has wept at tales of innocence distrest ;
> Her modest looks the cottage might adorn,
> Sweet as the primrose peeps beneath the thorn ;
> Now lost to all ; her friends, her virtue fled,
> Near her betrayer's door she lays her head.
> And, pinch'd with cold, and shrinking from the shower,
> With heavy heart deplores that luckless hour,
> When idly first, ambitious of the town,
> She left her wheel and robes of country brown."

Goldsmith wrote in a pre-Wordsworthian age, when,
even in the realms of poetry, a primrose was not much
more than a primrose ; but it is doubtful whether, either
before, during, or since Wordsworth's time the senti-
ment that the imagination can infuse into the common
and familiar things around us ever received more happy
expression than in the well-known line,

> " *Sweet as the primrose peeps beneath the thorn.*"

No one has as yet succeeded in defining accurately and
concisely what poetry is ; but at all events this line is
surcharged with a certain quality which is conspicuously
absent in such a production as the *Essay on Man.*
Another similar line is to be found further on in the
description of the distant scenes to which the proscribed
people are driven :

"Through torrid tracts with fainting steps they go,
Where wild Altama murmurs to their woe."

Indeed, the pathetic side of emigration has never been
so powerfully presented to us as in this poem—

"When the poor exiles, every pleasure past,
Hung round the bowers, and fondly looked their last,
And took a long farewell, and wished in vain
For seats like these beyond the western main,
And shuddering still to face the distant deep,
Returned and wept, and still returned to weep.

Even now, methinks, as pondering here I stand,
I see the rural virtues leave the land.
Down where yon anchoring vessel spreads the sail,
That idly waiting flaps with every gale,
Downward they move a melancholy band,
Pass from the shore, and darken all the strand.
Contented toil, and hospitable care,
And kind connubial tenderness are there ;
And piety with wishes placed above,
And steady loyalty, and faithful love."

And worst of all, in this imaginative departure, we find
that Poetry herself is leaving our shores. She is now to
try her voice

"On Torno's cliffs or Pambamarca's side ; "

and the poet, in the closing lines of the poem, bids her
a passionate and tender farewell :—

"And thou, sweet Poetry, thou loveliest maid,
Still first to fly where sensual joys invade ;

Unfit in these degenerate times of shame
To catch the heart, or strike for honest fame ;
Dear charming nymph, neglected and decried,
My shame in crowds, my solitary pride ;
Thou source of all my bliss, and all my woe,
That found'st me poor at first, and keep'st me so ;
Thou guide by which the nobler arts excel,
Thou nurse of every virtue, fare thee well !
Farewell, and O ! where'er thy voice be tried,
On Torno's cliffs, or Pambamarca's side,
Whether where equinoctial fervours glow,
Or winter wraps the polar world in snow,
Still let thy voice, prevailing over time,
Redress the rigours of the inclement clime ;
Aid slighted truth with thy persuasive strain ;
Teach erring man to spurn the rage of gain :
Teach him, that states of native strength possest,
Though very poor, may still be very blest ;
That trade's proud empire hastes to swift decay,
As ocean sweeps the laboured mole away ;
While self-dependent power can time defy,
As rocks resist the billows and the sky."

So ends this graceful, melodious, tender poem, the position of which in English literature, and in the estimation of all who love English literature, has not been disturbed by any fluctuations of literary fashion. We may give more attention at the moment to the new experiments of the poetic method ; but we return only with renewed gratitude to the old familiar strain, not the least merit of which is that it has nothing about it of foreign tricks or graces.   In English literature there is nothing more thoroughly English than these writings produced by an Irishman.   And whether or not it was Paddy Byrne, and Catherine Geraghty, and the Lissoy ale-house that

Goldsmith had in his mind when he was writing the poem, is not of much consequence : the manner and language and feeling are all essentially English ; so that we never think of calling Goldsmith anything but an English poet.

The poem met with great and immediate success. Of course everything that Dr. Goldsmith now wrote was read by the public ; he had not to wait for the recommendation of the reviews ; but, in this case, even the reviews had scarcely anything but praise in the welcome of his new book. It was dedicated, in graceful and ingenious terms, to Sir Joshua Reynolds, who returned the compliment by painting a picture and placing on the engraving of it this inscription : "This attempt to express a character in the *Deserted Village* is dedicated to Dr. Goldsmith by his sincere friend and admirer, Sir Joshua Reynolds." What Goldsmith got from Griffin for the poem is not accurately known ; and this is a misfortune, for the knowledge would have enabled us to judge whether at that time it was possible for a poet to court the draggle-tail muses without risk of starvation. But if fame were his chief object in the composition of the poem, he was sufficiently rewarded ; and it is to be surmised that by this time the people in Ireland—no longer implored to get subscribers—had heard of the proud position won by the vagrant youth who had "taken the world for his pillow" some eighteen years before.

That his own thoughts had sometimes wandered back to the scenes and friends of his youth during this labour of love, we know from his letters. In January of this year, while as yet the *Deserted*

K 2

Village was not quite through the press, he wrote
to his brother Maurice; and expressed himself as most
anxious to hear all about the relatives from whom he
had been so long parted.　He has something to say
about himself too; wishes it to be known that the King
has lately been pleased to make him Professor of Ancient
History "in a Royal Academy of Painting which he has
just established;" but gives no very flourishing account
of his circumstances.　"Honours to one in my situation
are something like ruffles to a man that wants a shirt."
However, there is some small legacy of fourteen or
fifteen pounds left him by his uncle Contarine, which
he understands to be in the keeping of his cousin
Lawder; and to this wealth he is desirous of foregoing
all claim : his relations must settle how it may be best
expended.　But there is not a reference to his literary
achievements, or the position won by them; not the
slightest yielding to even a pardonable vanity; it is a
modest, affectionate letter.　The only hint that Maurice
Goldsmith receives of the esteem in which his brother
is held in London, is contained in a brief mention of
Johnson, Burke, and others as his friends.　"I have
sent my cousin Jenny a miniature picture of myself,
as I believe it is the most acceptable present I can offer.
I have ordered it to be left for her at George Faulkenor's,
folded in a letter.　The face, you well know, is ugly
enough; but it is finely painted.　I will shortly also
send my friends over the Shannon some mezzotinto
prints of myself, and some more of my friends here,
such as Burke, Johnson, Reynolds, and Colman.　I
believe I have written an hundred letters to different
friends in your country, and never received an answer

from any of them. I do not know how to account for this, or why they are unwilling to keep up for me those regards which I must ever retain for them." The letter winds up with an appeal for news, news, news.

CHAPTER XV.

SOME two months after the publication of the *Deserted Village*, when its success had been well assured, Goldsmith proposed to himself the relaxation of a little Continental tour; and he was accompanied by three ladies, Mrs. Horneck and her two pretty daughters, who doubtless took more charge of him than he did of them. This Mrs. Horneck, the widow of a certain Captain Horneck, was connected with Reynolds, while Burke was the guardian of the two girls; so that it was natural that they should make the acquaintance of Dr. Goldsmith. A foolish attempt has been made to weave out of the relations supposed to exist between the younger of the girls and Goldsmith an imaginary romance; but there is not the slightest actual foundation for anything of the kind. Indeed the best guide we can have to the friendly and familiar terms on which he stood with regard to the Hornecks and their circle, is the following careless and jocular reply to a chance invitation sent him by the two sisters :—

> " Your mandate I got,
>   You may all go to pot;

Had your senses been right,
You'd have sent before night :
As I hope to be saved,
I put off being shaved ;
For I could not make bold,
While the matter was cold,
To meddle in suds,
Or to put on my duds ;
So tell Horneck and Nesbitt
And Baker and his bit,
And Kauffman beside,
And the Jessamy bride ;
With the rest of the crew,
The Reynoldses two,
Little Comedy's face
And the Captain in lace.

    ✿   ✿   ✿   ✿

Yet how can I when vext
Thus stray from my text ?
Tell each other to rue
Your Devonshire crew,
For sending so late
To one of my state.
But 'tis Reynolds's way
From wisdom to stray,
And Angelica's whim
To be frolic like him.

But, alas ! your good worships, how could they be wiser,
When both have been spoiled in to-day's *Advertiser ?* "

" The Jessamy Bride " was the pet nickname he had
bestowed on the younger Miss Horneck—the heroine of
the speculative romance just mentioned ; " Little
Comedy " was her sister ; " the Captain in lace " their
brother, who was in the Guards. No doubt Mrs.
Horneck and her daughters were very pleased to have

with them on this Continental trip so distinguished a
person as Dr. Goldsmith; and he must have been
very ungrateful if he was not glad to be provided with
such charming companions. The story of the sudden
envy he displayed of the admiration excited by the two
handsome young Englishwomen as they stood at a
hotel-window in Lille, is so incredibly foolish that it
needs scarcely be repeated here; unless to repeat the
warning that, if ever anybody was so dense as not to
see the humour of that piece of acting, one had better
look with grave suspicion on every one of the stories
told about Goldsmith's vanities and absurdities.

Even with such pleasant companions, the trip to Paris
was not everything he had hoped. " I find," he wrote
to Reynolds from Paris, " that travelling at twenty and
at forty are very different things. I set out with all
my confirmed habits about me, and can find nothing
on the Continent so good as when I formerly left it.
One of our chief amusements here is scolding at everything we meet with, and praising every thing and every
person we left at home. You may judge therefore
whether your name is not frequently bandied at table
among us. To tell you the truth, I never thought I
could regret your absence so much, as our various
mortifications on the road have often taught me to do.
I could tell you of disasters and adventures without
number, of our lying in barns, and of my being half
poisoned with a dish of green peas, of our quarrelling
with postilions and being cheated by our landladies, but
I reserve all this for a happy hour which I expect to
share with you upon my return." The fact is that
although Goldsmith had seen a good deal of foreign

travel, the manner of his making the grand tour in his youth was not such as to fit him for acting as courier to a party of ladies. However, if they increased his troubles, they also shared them ; and in this same letter he bears explicit testimony to the value of their companionship. " I will soon be among you, better pleased with my situation at home than I ever was before. And yet I must say, that if anything could make France pleasant, the very good women with whom I am at present would certainly do it. I could say more about that, but I intend showing them this letter before I send it away." Mrs. Horneck, Little Comedy, the Jessamy Bride, and the Professor of Ancient History at the Royal Academy, all returned to London ; the last to resume his round of convivialities at taverns, excursions into regions of more fashionable amusement along with Reynolds, and task-work aimed at the pockets of the booksellers.

It was a happy-go-lucky sort of life. We find him now showing off his fine clothes and his sword and wig at Ranelagh Gardens, and again shut up in his chambers compiling memoirs and histories in hot haste ; now the guest of Lord Clare, and figuring at Bath, and again delighting some small domestic circle by his quips and cranks ; playing jokes for the amusement of children, and writing comic letters in verse to their elders ; everywhere and at all times merry, thoughtless, good-natured. And, of course, we find also his humorous pleasantries being mistaken for blundering stupidity. In perfect good faith Boswell describes how a number of people burst out laughing when Goldsmith publicly complained that he had met Lord Camden at Lord

Clare's house in the country, "and he took no more notice of me than if I had been an ordinary man." Goldsmith's claiming to be a very extraordinary person was precisely a stroke of that humorous self-depreciation in which he was continually indulging; and the Jessamy Bride has left it on record that "on many occasions, from the peculiar manner of his humour, and assumed frown of countenance, what was often uttered in jest was mistaken by those who did not know him for earnest." This would appear to have been one of those occasions. The company burst out laughing at Goldsmith's having made a fool of himself; and Johnson was compelled to come to his rescue. "Nay, gentlemen, Dr. Goldsmith is in the right. A nobleman ought to have made up to such a man as Goldsmith; and I think it is much against Lord Camden that he neglected him."

Mention of Lord Clare naturally recalls the *Haunch of Venison*. Goldsmith was particularly happy in writing bright and airy verses; the grace and lightness of his touch has rarely been approached. It must be confessed, however, that in this direction he was somewhat of an Autolycus; unconsidered trifles he freely appropriated; but he committed these thefts with scarcely any concealment, and with the most charming air in the world. In fact some of the snatches of verse which he contributed to the *Bee* scarcely profess to be anything else than translations, though the originals are not given. But who is likely to complain when we get as the result such a delightful piece of nonsense as the famous Elegy on that Glory of her Sex, Mrs. Mary Blaize, which has been the parent of a vast progeny since Goldsmith's time?

" Good people all, with one accord
    Lament for Madam Blaize,
Who never wanted a good word,
    From those who spoke her praise.

" The needy seldom passed her door,
    And always found her kind ;
She freely lent to all the poor,—
    Who left a pledge behind.

" She strove the neighbourhood to please,
    With manners wondrous winning ;
And never followed wicked ways,—
    Unless when she was sinning.

" At church, in silks and satins new,
    With hoop of monstrous size,
She never slumbered in her pew,—
    But when she shut her eyes.

" Her love was sought, I do aver,
    By twenty beaux and more ;
The king himself has followed her,—
    When she has walked before.

" But now her wealth and finery fled,
    Her hangers-on cut short all ;
The doctors found, when she was dead,—
    Her last disorder mortal.

" Let us lament, in sorrow sore,
    For Kent Street well may say,
That had she lived a twelvemonth more,—
    She had not died to-day."

The *Haunch of Venison*, on the other hand, is a poetical
letter of thanks to Lord Clare—an easy, jocular epistle,
in which the writer has a cut or two at certain of his
literary brethren. Then, as he is looking at the venison,

and determining not to send it to any such people as
Hiffernan or Higgins, who should step in but our old
friend Beau Tibbs, or some one remarkably like him in
manner and speech ?—

> " While thus I debated, in reverie centred,
>   An acquaintance, a friend as he called himself, entered ;
>   An under-bred, fine-spoken fellow was he,
>   And he smiled as he looked at the venison and me.
>   ' What have we got here ?—Why this is good eating !
>   Your own, I suppose—or is it in waiting ? '
>   ' Why, whose should it be ? ' cried I with a flounce ;
>   ' I get these things often '—but that was a bounce :
>   ' Some lords, my acquaintance, that settle the nation,
>   Are pleased to be kind—but I hate ostentation.'
>   ' If that be the case then,' cried he, very gay,
>   ' I'm glad I have taken this house in my way.
>   To-morrow you take a poor dinner with me ;
>   No words—I insist on't—precisely at three ;
>   We'll have Johnson, and Burke ; all the wits will be there ;
>   My acquaintance is slight, or I'd ask my Lord Clare.
>   And now that I think on't, as I am a sinner !
>   We wanted this venison to make out the dinner.
>   What say you—a pasty ?   It shall, and it must,
>   And my wife, little Kitty, is famous for crust.
>   Here, porter ! this venison with me to Mile End ;
>   No stirring—I beg—my dear friend—my dear friend ! '
>   Thus, snatching his hat, he brushed off like the wind,
>   And the porter and eatables followed behind."

We need not follow the vanished venison—which did
not make its appearance at the banquet any more than
did Johnson or Burke—further than to say that if Lord
Clare did not make it good to the poet he did not deserve
to have his name associated with such a clever and
careless *jeu d'esprit.*

CHAPTER XVI.

SHE STOOPS TO CONQUER.

BUT the writing of smart verses could not keep
Dr. Goldsmith alive, more especially as dinner-
parties, Ranelagh masquerades, and similar diversions
pressed heavily on his finances. When his *History of
England* appeared, the literary cut-throats of the day
accused him of having been bribed by the Government
to betray the liberties of the people : [1] a foolish charge.
What Goldsmith got for the *English History* was the
sum originally stipulated for, and now no doubt all
spent ; with a further sum of fifty guineas for an
abridgment of the work. Then, by this time, he had
persuaded Griffin to advance him the whole of the
eight hundred guineas for the *Animated Nature*, though
he had only done about a third part of the book. At
the instigation of Newbery he had begun a story after
the manner of the *Vicar of Wakefield ;* but it appears
that such chapters as he had written were not deemed

[1] " God knows I had no thought for or against liberty in my head ;
my whole aim being to make up a book of a decent size that, as
Squire Richard says, ' would do no harm to nobody.' "—Goldsmith
to Langton, September, 1771.

to be promising; and the undertaking was abandoned. The fact is, Goldsmith was now thinking of another method of replenishing his purse. The *Vicar of Wakefield* had brought him little but reputation; the *Good-natured Man* had brought him £500. It was to the stage that he now looked for assistance out of the financial slough in which he was plunged. He was engaged in writing a comedy; and that comedy was *She Stoops to Conquer*.

In the Dedication to Johnson which was prefixed to this play on its appearance in type, Goldsmith hints that the attempt to write a comedy not of the sentimental order then in fashion, was a hazardous thing; and also that Colman, who saw the piece in its various stages, was of this opinion too. Colman threw cold water on the undertaking from the very beginning. It was only extreme pressure on the part of Goldsmith's friends that induced—or rather compelled—him to accept the comedy; and that, after he had kept the unfortunate author in the tortures of suspense for month after month. But although Goldsmith knew the danger, he was resolved to face it. He hated the sentimentalists and all their works; and determined to keep his new comedy faithful to nature, whether people called it low or not. His object was to raise a genuine, hearty laugh; not to write a piece for school declamation; and he had enough confidence in himself to do the work in his own way. Moreover he took the earliest possible opportunity, in writing this piece, of poking fun at the sensitive creatures who had been shocked by the "vulgarity" of *The Good-natured Man*. "Bravo! Bravo!" cry the jolly companions of Tony Lumpkin, when that promising buckeen

has finished his song at the Three Pigeons ; then follows
criticism :—

"*First Fellow.* The squire has got spunk in him.

Second Fel. I loves to hear him sing, bekeays he never gives
us nothing that's low.

Third Fel. O damn anything that's low, I cannot bear it.

Fourth Fel. The genteel thing is the genteel thing any
time : if so be that a gentleman bees in a concatenation
accordingly.

Third Fel. I likes the maxum of it, Master Muggins.
What, though I am obligated to dance a bear, a man may be
a gentleman for all that.   May this be my poison, if my bear
ever dances but to the very genteelest of tunes ; ' Water
Parted,' or the ' The Minuet in Ariadne.' "

Indeed, Goldsmith, however he might figure in society,
was always capable of holding his own when he had his
pen in his hand.   And even at the outset of this comedy
one sees how much he has gained in literary confidence
since the writing of the *Good-natured Man.*   Here
there is no anxious stiffness at all ; but a brisk, free
conversation, full of point that is not too formal, and
yet conveying all the information that has usually to be
crammed into a first scene.   In taking as the ground-
work of his plot that old adventure that had befallen
himself—his mistaking a squire's house for an inn—he
was hampering himself with something that was not the
less improbable because it had actually happened ; but
we begin to forget all the improbabilities through the
naturalness of the people to whom we are introduced,
and the brisk movement and life of the piece.

Fashions in dramatic literature may come and go ; but
the wholesome good-natured fun of *She Stoops to Conquer*

is as capable of producing a hearty laugh now, as it was when it first saw the light in Covent Garden. Tony Lumpkin is one of the especial favourites of the theatre-going public; and no wonder. With all the young cub's jibes and jeers, his impudence and grimaces, one has a sneaking love for the scapegrace; we laugh with him, rather than at him; how can we fail to enjoy those malevolent tricks of his when he so obviously enjoys them himself? And Diggory—do we not owe an eternal debt of gratitude to honest Diggory for telling us about Ould Grouse in the gunroom, that immortal joke at which thousands and thousands of people have roared with laughter, though they never any one of them could tell what the story was about? The scene in which the old squire lectures his faithful attendants on their manners and duties, is one of the truest bits of comedy on the English stage:

"*Mr. Hardcastle.* But you're not to stand so, with your hands in your pockets. Take your hands from your pockets, Roger; and from your head, you blockhead you. See how Diggory carries his hands. They're a little too stiff, indeed, but that's no great matter.

Diggory. Ay, mind how I hold them. I learned to hold my hands this way when I was upon drill for the militia. And so being upon drill——

Hard. You must not be so talkative, Diggory. You must be all attention to the guests. You must hear us talk, and not think of talking; you must see us drink, and not think of drinking; you must see us eat, and not think of eating.

Dig. By the laws, your worship, that's perfectly unpossible, Whenever Diggory sees yeating going forward, ecod, he's always wishing for a mouthful himself.

Hard. Blockhead ! Is not a bellyfull in the kitchen as good as a bellyfull in the parlour ? Stay your stomach with that reflection.

Dig. Ecod, I thank your worship, I'll make a shift to stay my stomach with a slice of cold beef in the pantry.

Hard. Diggory, you are too talkative.—Then, if I happen to say a good thing, or tell a good story at table, you must not all burst out a-laughing, as if you made part of the company.

Dig. Then ecod your worship must not tell the story of Ould Grouse in the gunroom : I can't help laughing at that —he ! he ! he !—for the soul of me. We have laughed at that these twenty years—ha ! ha ! ha !

Hard. Ha ! ha ! ha ! The story is a good one. Well, honest Diggory, you may laugh at that—but still remember to be attentive. Suppose one of the company should call for a glass of wine, how will you behave ? A glass of wine, sir, if you please (*to* DIGGORY).—Eh, why don't you move ?

Dig. Ecod, your worship, I never have courage till I see the eatables and drinkables brought upo' the table, and then I'm as bauld as a lion.

Hard. What, will nobody move ?

First Serv. I'm not to leave this pleace.

Second Serv. I'm sure it's no pleace of mine.

Third Serv. Nor mine, for sartain.

Dig. Wauns, and I'm sure it canna be mine."

No doubt all this is very "low" indeed ; and perhaps Mr. Colman may be forgiven for suspecting that the refined wits of the day would be shocked by these rude humours of a parcel of servants. But all that can be said in this direction was said at the time by Horace Walpole, in a letter to a friend of his ; and this criticism is so amusing in its pretence and imbecility that it is worth quoting at large. " Dr. Goldsmith has written a comedy," says this profound critic, " — no, it is the

L

lowest of all farces; it is not the subject I condemn,
though very vulgar, but the execution. The drift tends
to no moral, no edification of any kind—the situations,
however, are well imagined, and make one laugh in spite
of the grossness of the dialogue, the forced witticisms,
and total improbability of the whole plan and conduct.
But what disgusts me most is, that though the characters
are very low, and aim at low humour, not one of them
says a sentence that is natural, or marks any character
at all."   Horace Walpole sighing for edification—from a
Covent Garden comedy !   Surely, if the old gods have
any laughter left, and if they take any notice of what
is done in the literary world here below, there must
have rumbled through the courts of Olympus a guffaw of
sardonic laughter, when that solemn criticism was put
down on paper.

Meanwhile Colman's original fears had developed into
a sort of stupid obstinacy. He was so convinced that
the play would not succeed, that he would spend no
money in putting it on the stage; while far and wide he
announced its failure as a foregone conclusion. Under
this gloom of vaticination the rehearsals were nevertheless proceeded with—the brunt of the quarrels among
the players falling wholly on Goldsmith, for the manager
seems to have withdrawn in despair ; while all the
Johnson confraternity were determined to do what they
could for Goldsmith on the opening night. That was the
15th of March, 1773. His friends invited the author to
dinner as a prelude to the play ; Dr. Johnson was in the
chair ; there was plenty of gaiety. But this means of
keeping up the anxious author's spirits was not very successful. Goldsmith's mouth, we are told by Reynolds,

became so parched "from the agitation of his mind, that he was unable to swallow a single mouthful." Moreover, he could not face the ordeal of sitting through the play; when his friends left the tavern and betook themselves to the theatre, he went away by himself; and was subsequently found walking in St. James's Park. The friend who discovered him there, persuaded him that his presence in the theatre might be useful in case of an emergency; and ultimately got him to accompany him to Covent Garden. When Goldsmith reached the theatre, the fifth act had been begun.

Oddly enough, the first thing he heard on entering the stage-door was a hiss. The story goes that the poor author was dreadfully frightened; and that in answer to a hurried question, Colman exclaimed, "Psha! Doctor, don't be afraid of a squib, when we have been sitting these two hours on a barrel of gunpowder." If this was meant as a hoax, it was a cruel one; if meant seriously, it was untrue. For the piece had turned out a great hit. From beginning to end of the performance the audience were in a roar of laughter; and the single hiss that Goldsmith unluckily heard was so markedly exceptional, that it became the talk of the town, and was variously attributed to one or other of Goldsmith's rivals. Colman, too, suffered at the hands of the wits for his gloomy and falsified predictions; and had, indeed, to beg Goldsmith to intercede for him. It is a great pity that Boswell was not in London at this time; for then we might have had a description of the supper that naturally would follow the play, and of Goldsmith's demeanour under this new success. Besides the gratification, moreover, of his choice of materials being approved by the public, there was the material benefit accruing to him from the three "author's nights." These are supposed to have produced nearly five hundred pounds—a substantial sum in those days.

Boswell did not come to London till the second of April following ; and the first mention we find of Goldsmith is in connection with an incident which has its ludicrous as well as its regrettable aspect.   The further success of *She Stoops to Conquer* was not likely to propitiate the wretched hole-and-corner cut-throats that infested the journalism of that day.   More especially was Kenrick driven mad with envy ; and so, in a letter addressed to the *London Packet,* this poor creature determined once more to set aside the judgment of the public, and show Dr. Goldsmith in his true colours.   The letter is a wretched production, full of personalities only fit for an angry washerwoman, and of rancour without point.   But there was one passage in it that effectually roused Goldsmith's rage ; for here the Jessamy Bride was introduced as " the lovely H—k." The letter was anonymous ; but the publisher of the print, a man called Evans, was known ; and so Goldsmith thought he would go and give Evans a beating.   If he had asked Johnson's advice about the matter, he would no doubt have been told to pay no heed at all to anonymous scurrility—certainly not to attempt to reply to it with a cudgel.   When Johnson heard that Foote meant to " take him off," he turned to Davies and asked him what was the common price of an oak stick ; but an oak stick in Johnson's hands, and an oak stick in Goldsmith's hands, were two different things.   However, to the bookseller's shop the indignant poet proceeded, in company with a friend; got hold of Evans; accused him of having insulted a young lady by putting her name in his paper; and, when the publisher would fain have shifted the responsibility on to the editor, forthwith denounced him as a rascal, and hit him over the back with his cane. The publisher, however, was quite a match for Goldsmith; and there is no saying how the deadly combat might have ended, had not a lamp been broken overhead, the oil of which drenched both the warriors. This intervention of the superior gods was just as successful as a Homeric cloud; the fray ceased; Goldsmith and his friend withdrew; and ultimately an action for assault was compromised by Goldsmith's paying fifty pounds to a charity. Then the howl of the journals arose. Their prerogative had been assailed. "Attacks upon private character were the most liberal existing source of newspaper income," Mr. Forster writes; and so the pack turned with one cry on the unlucky poet. There was nothing of "the Monument" about poor Goldsmith; and at last he was worried into writing a letter of defence addressed to the public. "He has indeed done it very well," said Johnson to Boswell, "but it is a foolish thing well done." And further he remarked, "Why, sir, I believe it is the first time he has *beat;* he may have *been beaten* before. This, sir, is a new plume to him."

CHAPTER XVII.

INCREASING DIFFICULTIES.—THE END.

THE pecuniary success of *She Stoops to Conquer* did
but little to relieve Goldsmith from those financial
embarrassments which were now weighing heavily on his
mind. And now he had less of the old high spirits that
had enabled him to laugh off the cares of debt. His
health became disordered ; an old disease renewed its
attacks, and was grown more violent because of his
long-continued sedentary habits. Indeed, from this
point to the day of his death—not a long interval,
either—we find little but a record of successive endeavours, some of them wild and hopeless enough, to
obtain money anyhow. Of course he went to the Club,
as usual ; and gave dinner-parties ; and had a laugh or
a song ready for the occasion. It is possible, also, to
trace a certain growth of confidence in himself, no
doubt the result of the repeated proofs of his genius
he had put before his friends. It was something more
than mere personal intimacy that justified the rebuke
he administered to Reynolds, when the latter painted an
allegorical picture representing the triumph of Beattie
and Truth over Voltaire and Scepticism. " It very ill

becomes a man of your eminence and character," he said, " to debase so high a genius as Voltaire before so mean a writer as Beattie. Beattie and his book will be forgotten in ten years, while Voltaire's fame will last for ever. Take care it does not perpetuate this picture, to the shame of such a man as you." He was aware, too, of the position he had won for himself in English literature. He knew that people in after-days would ask about him ; and it was with no sort of unwarrantable vainglory that he gave Percy certain materials for a biography which he wished him to undertake. Hence the *Percy Memoir*.

He was only forty-five when he made this request ; and he had not suffered much from illness during his life ; so that there was apparently no grounds for imagining that the end was near. But at this time Goldsmith began to suffer severe fits of depression ; and he grew irritable and capricious of temper—no doubt another result of failing health. He was embroiled in disputes with the booksellers ; and, on one occasion, seems to have been much hurt because Johnson, who had been asked to step in as arbiter, decided against him. He was offended with Johnson on another occasion because of his sending away certain dishes at a dinner given to him by Goldsmith, as a hint that these entertainments were too luxurious for one in Goldsmith's position. It was probably owing to some temporary feeling of this sort—perhaps to some expression of it on Goldsmith's part—that Johnson spoke of Goldsmith's " malice " towards him. Mrs. Thrale had suggested that Goldsmith would be the best person to write Johnson's biography. "The dog would write it best, to be sure,"

said Johnson, " but his particular malice towards me,
and general disregard of truth, would make the book
useless to all and injurious to my character." Of course
it is always impossible to say what measure of jocular
exaggeration there may not be in a chance phrase such
as this : of the fact that there was no serious or permanent quarrel between the two friends we have abundant
proof in Boswell's faithful pages.

To return to the various endeavours made by Goldsmith and his friends to meet the difficulties now
closing in around him, we find, first of all, the familiar
hack-work. For two volumes of a *History of Greece*
he had received from Griffin £250. Then his friends
tried to get him a pension from the Government; but
this was definitely refused. An expedient of his own
seemed to promise well at first. He thought of bringing
out a *Popular Dictionary of Arts and Sciences*, a series
of contributions mostly by his friends, with himself as
editor ; and among those who offered to assist him were
Johnson, Reynolds, Burke, and Dr. Burney. But the
booksellers were afraid. The project would involve a
large expense ; and they had no high opinion of Goldsmith's business habits. Then he offered to alter *The
Good-natured Man* for Garrick ; but Garrick preferred
to treat with him for a new comedy, and generously
allowed him to draw on him for the money in advance.
This last help enabled him to go to Barton for a brief
holiday; but the relief was only temporary. On his
return to London even his nearest friends began to
observe the change in his manner. In the old days
Goldsmith had faced pecuniary difficulties with a light
heart ; but now, his health broken, and every avenue

of escape apparently closed, he was giving way to despair. His friend Cradock, coming up to town, found Goldsmith in a most despondent condition ; and also hints that the unhappy author was trying to conceal the true state of affairs. " I believe," says Cradock, " he died miserable, and that his friends were not entirely aware of his distress."

And yet it was during this closing period of anxiety, despondency, and gloomy foreboding, that the brilliant and humorous lines of *Retaliation* were written—that last scintillation of the bright and happy genius that was soon to be extinguished for ever. The most varied accounts have been given of the origin of this *jeu d'esprit ;* and even Garrick's, which was meant to supersede and correct all others, is self-contradictory. For according to this version of the story, which was found among the Garrick papers, and which is printed in Mr. Cunningham's edition of Goldsmith's works, the whole thing arose out of Goldsmith and Garrick resolving one evening at the St. James's Coffee House to write each other's epitaph. Garrick's well-known couplet was instantly produced :

> " Here lies Nolly Goldsmith, for shortness called Noll,
> Who wrote like an angel, but talked like poor Poll."

Goldsmith, according to Garrick, either would not or could not retort at the moment ; " but went to work, and some weeks after produced the following printed poem, called *Retaliation.*" But Garrick himself goes on to say, " The following poems in manuscript were written by several of the gentlemen on purpose to provoke the

Doctor to an answer, which came forth at last with great
credit to him in *Retaliation*." The most probable
version of the story, which may be pieced together from
various sources, is that at the coffee-house named this
business of writing comic epitaphs was started some
evening or other by the whole company; that Goldsmith
and Garrick pitted themselves against each other; that
thereafter Goldsmith began as occasion served to write
similar squibs about his friends, which were shown
about as they were written; that thereupon those
gentlemen, not to be behindhand, composed more
elaborate pieces in proof of their wit; and that, finally,
Goldsmith resolved to bind these fugitive lines of his
together in a poem, which he left unfinished, and which,
under the name of *Retaliation*, was published after his
death. This hypothetical account receives some con-
firmation from the fact that the scheme of the poem and
its component parts do not fit together well; the introduction looks like an after-thought; and has not the
freedom and pungency of a piece of improvisation. An
imaginary dinner is described, the guests being Garrick,
Reynolds, Burke, Cumberland, and the rest of them,
Goldsmith last of all. More wine is called for, until
the whole of his companions have fallen beneath the
table :

> " Then, with chaos and blunders encircling my head,
>   Let me ponder, and tell what I think of the *dead*."

This is a somewhat clumsy excuse for introducing a
series of epitaphs; but the epitaphs amply atone for it.
That on Garrick is especially remarkable as a bit of

character-sketching ; its shrewd hints—all in perfect
courtesy and good humour—going a little nearer to the
truth than is common in epitaphs of any sort :—

> " Here lies David Garrick, describe me who can ;
> An abridgment of all that was pleasant in man.
> As an actor, confessed without rival to shine :
> As a wit, if not first, in the very first line :
> Yet, with talents like these, and an excellent heart,
> The man had his failings, a dupe to his art.
> Like an ill-judging beauty, his colours he spread,
> And beplastered with rouge his own natural red.
> On the stage he was natural, simple, affecting ;
> 'Twas only that, when he was off, he was acting.
> With no reason on earth to go out of his way,
> He turned and he varied full ten times a day :
> Though secure of our hearts, yet confoundedly sick
> If they were not his own by finessing and trick ;
> He cast off his friends, as a huntsman his pack,
> For he knew when he pleased he could whistle them back.
> Of praise a mere glutton, he swallowed what came ;
> And the puff of a dunce, he mistook it for fame ;
> Till his relish grown callous, almost to disease,
> Who peppered the highest was surest to please.
> But let us be candid, and speak out our mind :
> If dunces applauded, he paid them in kind.
> Ye Kenricks, ye Kellys, and Woodfalls so grave,
> What a commerce was yours, while you got and you gave !
> How did Grub Street re-echo the shouts that you raised,
> While he was be-Rosciused, and you were bepraised.
> But peace to his spirit, wherever it flies,
> To act as an angel and mix with the skies :
> Those poets who owe their best fame to his skill
> Shall still be his flatterers, go where he will ;
> Old Shakespeare receive him with praise and with love,
> And Beaumonts and Bens be his Kellys above."

The truth is that Goldsmith, though he was ready to bless his "honest little man" when he received from him sixty pounds in advance for a comedy not begun, never took quite so kindly to Garrick as to some of his other friends. There is no pretence of discrimination at all, for example, in the lines devoted in this poem to Reynolds. All the generous enthusiasm of Goldsmith's Irish nature appears here; he will admit of no possible rival to this especial friend of his :—

> " Here Reynolds is laid, and to tell you my mind,
> He has not left a wiser or better behind."

There is a tradition that the epitaph on Reynolds, ending with the unfinished line

> " By flattery unspoiled ₒ ₒ ₒ "

was Goldsmith's last piece of writing. One would like to believe that, in any case.

Goldsmith had returned to his Edgware lodgings, and had, indeed, formed some notion of selling his chambers in the Temple, and living in the country for at least ten months in the year, when a sudden attack of his old disorder drove him into town again for medical advice. He would appear to have received some relief; but a nervous fever followed; and on the night of the 25th March, 1774, when he was but forty-six years of age, he took to his bed for the last time. At first he refused to regard his illness as serious; and insisted on dosing himself with certain fever-powders from which he had received benefit on previous occasions; but by and by as his strength gave way, he submitted to the advice of the physicians who were in attendance on him. Day

after day passed ; his weakness visibly increasing,
though, curiously enough, the symptoms of fever were
gradually abating. At length one of the doctors, remarking to him that his pulse was in greater disorder
than it should be from the degree of fever, asked him
if his mind was at ease. "No, it is not," answered
Goldsmith; and these were his last words. Early in
the morning of Monday, April 4, convulsions set in ;
these continued for rather more than an hour ; then the
troubled brain and the sick heart found rest for ever.

When the news was carried to his friends, Burke, it
is said, burst into tears, and Reynolds put aside his
work for the day. But it does not appear that they
had visited him during his illness ; and neither Johnson,
nor Reynolds, nor Burke, nor Garrick followed his body
to the grave. It is true, a public funeral was talked of ;
and, among others, Reynolds, Burke, and Garrick were
to have carried the pall ; but this was abandoned ; and
Goldsmith was privately buried in the ground of the
Temple Church on the 9th of April, 1774. Strangely
enough, too, Johnson seems to have omitted all mention
of Goldsmith from his letters to Boswell. It was not
until Boswell had written to him, on June 24th, " You
have said nothing to me about poor Goldsmith," that
Johnson, writing on July 4, answered as follows :—
"Of poor dear Dr. Goldsmith there is little to be
told, more than the papers have made public. He died
of a fever, made, I am afraid, more violent by uneasiness of mind. His debts began to be heavy, and all
his resources were exhausted. Sir Joshua is of opinion
that he owed not less than two thousand pounds. Was
ever poet so trusted before ? "

But if the greatest grief at the sudden and premature
death of Goldsmith would seem to have been shown
at the moment by certain wretched creatures who were
found weeping on the stairs leading to his chambers, it
must not be supposed that his fine friends either forgot
him, or ceased to regard his memory with a great
gentleness and kindness.   Some two years after, when
a'monument was about to be erected to Goldsmith in
Westminster Abbey, Johnson consented to write "the
poor dear Doctor's epitaph;" and so anxious were the
members of that famous circle in which Goldsmith
had figured, that a just tribute should be paid to his
genius, that they even ventured to send a round robin
to the great Cham desiring him to amend his first
draft.   Now, perhaps, we have less interest in Johnson's estimate of Goldsmith's genius—though it contains the famous *Nullum quod tetigit non ornavit*—
than in the phrases which tell of the honour paid to
the memory of the dead poet by the love of his companions and the faithfulness of his friends.   It may
here be added that the precise spot where Goldsmith was
buried in the Temple churchyard is unknown.   So lived
and so died Oliver Goldsmith.

In the foregoing pages the writings of Goldsmith
have been given so prominent a place in the history
of his life that it is unnecessary to take them here
collectively and endeavour to sum up their distinc-
tive qualities.   As much as could be said within the
limited space has, it is hoped, been said about their
genuine and tender pathos, that never at any time

verges on the affected or theatrical ; about their quaint
delicate, delightful humour ; about that broader humour
that is not afraid to provoke the wholesome laughter of
mankind by dealing with common and familiar ways,
and manners, and men ; about that choiceness of diction,
that lightness and grace of touch, that lend a charm
even to Goldsmith's ordinary hack-work.

Still less necessary, perhaps, is it to review the facts
and circumstances of Goldsmith's life ; and to make of
them an example, a warning, or an accusation. That has
too often been done. His name has been used to glorify
a sham Bohemianism—a Bohemianism that finds it easy
to live in taverns, but does not find it easy, so far as
one sees, to write poems like the *Deserted Village*. His
experiences as an author have been brought forward to
swell the cry about neglected genius—that is, by writers
who assume their genius in order to prove the neglect.
The misery that occasionally befell him during his wayward career has been made the basis of an accusation
against society, the English constitution, Christianity—
Heaven knows what. It is time to have done with all
this nonsense. Goldsmith resorted to the hack-work of
literature when everything else had failed him ; and he
was fairly paid for it. When he did better work, when
he " struck for honest fame," the nation gave him all
the honour that he could have desired. With an assured
reputation, and with ample means of subsistence, he
obtained entrance into the most distinguished society
then in England—he was made the friend of England's
greatest in the arts and literature—and could have
confined himself to that society exclusively if he had
chosen. His temperament, no doubt, exposed him to

suffering; and the exquisite sensitiveness of a man of genius may demand our sympathy; but in far greater measure is our sympathy demanded for the thousands upon thousands of people who, from illness or nervous excitability, suffer from quite as keen a sensitiveness without the consolation of the fame that genius brings.

In plain truth, Goldsmith himself would have been the last to put forward pleas humiliating alike to himself and to his calling. Instead of beseeching the State to look after authors; instead of imploring society to grant them "recognition;" instead of saying of himself "he wrote, and paid the penalty;" he would frankly have admitted that he chose to live his life his own way, and therefore paid the penalty. This is not written with any desire of upbraiding Goldsmith. He did choose to live his own life his own way, and we now have the splendid and beautiful results of his work; and the world—looking at these with a constant admiration, and with a great and lenient love for their author—is not anxious to know what he did with his guineas, or whether the milkman was ever paid. "He had raised money and squandered it, by every artifice of acquisition and folly of expense. BUT LET NOT HIS FRAILTIES BE REMEMBERED : HE WAS A VERY GREAT MAN." This is Johnson's wise summing up; and with it we may here take leave of gentle Goldsmith.

THE END.

For EU product safety concerns, contact us at Calle de José Abascal, 56–1°,
28003 Madrid, Spain or eugpsr@cambridge.org.

www.ingramcontent.com/pod-product-compliance
Ingram Content Group UK Ltd.
Pitfield, Milton Keynes, MK11 3LW, UK
UKHW012341130625
459647UK00009B/450